F*CKING HISTORY

F*CKING HISTORY

111 LESSONS
You Should Have Learned in School

THE CAPTAIN

A TarcherPerigee Book

tarcherperigee

an imprint of Penguin Random House LLC
penguinrandomhouse.com

Most TarcherPerigee books are available at special quantity discounts for bulk purchase for sales promotions, premiums, fund-raising, and educational needs. Special books or book excerpts also can be created to fit specific needs.
For details, write: SpecialMarkets@penguinrandomhouse.com.

Library of Congress Cataloging-in-Publication Data

Names: Captain, The, author.
Title: F*cking history: 111 lessons you should have learned in school / The Captain.
Other titles: Fucking history
Description: New York: TarcherPerigee, Penguin Random House LLC, 2020.
Identifiers: LCCN 2020004961 (print) | LCCN 2020004962 (ebook) |
ISBN 9780593189412 (paperback) | ISBN 9780593189610 (ebook)
Subjects: LCSH: History—Humor. | History—Anecdotes.
Classification: LCC D10 .C329 2020 (print) | LCC D10 (ebook) |
DDC 902/.07—dc23
LC record available at https://lccn.loc.gov/2020004961
LC ebook record available at https://lccn.loc.gov/2020004962

Printed in the United States of America

1 3 5 7 9 10 8 6 4 2

Book design by Lorie Pagnozzi

Illustrations by Gary Bueno

Ashley, we're done.

CONTENTS

A NO-BULLSHIT BEGINNING   2

GETTIN' GHOSTED   4

TILL DEATH DO YOU PART (OR NOT)   6

HATERS GONNA HATE   8

TIMELESS BEAUTY   10

TWO'S A COUPLE, THREE'S A CROWD   12

STAGE FRIGHT, DIVORCE FIGHT   14

MEOWLESS AND BROWLESS   16

A CATFISH CRUSADE   18

KIS(S)MET   20

APPLE ALLURE 22

SQUAD GOALS 24

TOO MANY TO NAME 26

SETTLING IS A SLOW DEATH 28

THE STRAP OF WRATH 30

PIGGYBACKS SAVE LIVES 32

TEMPER TANTRUMS 34

REINVENTING YOURSELF 36

INFLUENCED BY AFFLUENCE 38

A TRULY LOYAL ROYAL 40

FEAR OF MISSING OUT 42

FAKE IT, SEE HOW THEY TAKE IT 44

SUPPORT YOURSELF 46

SHOW SOME RESPECT 48

FROM THE THEATRE TO THE THRONE 50

CROWN ON, CLAWS OUT 52

CAN'T TOUCH THIS 54

HE(A)DY TIMES IN HOLLYWOOD 56

KNOW WHEN TO GO   58

ON TIME AND HONORABLE   60

SEXUAL SWORDPLAY   62

SPREADING BLAME   64

A HEARTFELT AFFAIR   66

YOUR DOG KNOWS BEST   68

PARISIAN PROSTITUTION   70

DON'T LOSE SIGHT OF YOURSELF   72

OUTWIT AND OUTLIVE   74

A RIDE WORTH REMEMBERING   76

JAILHOUSE WEDLOCK   78

A HAIRY PROPOSITION   80

STEP YOUR GAME UP   82

ROMANTIC REVENGE   84

KEEP IT PRIVATE   86

A PROVOKING SMOKE   88

CRAZY-LADY BAY   90

GET IT, GIRL   92

FIGHTING FOR THE RIGHT 94

LAWS, LIARS, AND LIBATIONS 96

A MUTUAL UNDERSTANDING 98

P-P-P-P-POWER 100

PET PARENTING 101 102

BUCKET BRAWLERS 104

PROACTIVE POLITICS 106

FEMALE FEROCITY 108

NACHO DADDY 110

THE PIRATE QUEEN 112

TANK IT TO 'EM 114

LOOKIN' GOOD, HONEY 116

THE DEVIL FROM OHIO 118

SILENCE IS SO SKETCHY 120

BITING BACK 122

LOAF LOVE AS SELF-LOVE 124

PUSSY PLUNDER 126

DENIAL ON THE NILE 128

PLAYING WITH DOLLS	130
FEAR NOTHING, TAKE EVERYTHING	132
SISTERS STICK TOGETHER	134
PAINT YOUR OWN PATH	136
BLONDES HAVE MORE FUN	138
LEAVE AN IMPRESSION	140
THINK ABOUT IT	142
THE HEROINES OF HEATING	144
HORSESHOES AND HAND GRENADES	146
(WO)MAN OVERBOARD	148
THE JOKE'S ON THEM	150
SECRECY IS SACRED	152
ONE-SIDED SOBRIETY	154
THE MO(U)RNING AFTER	156
THE SMELL OF VICTORY	158
THINK FAST AND YOUR LEGEND MIGHT LAST	160
A STABBY STANDOFF	162
BATHING IN BELIEVABILITY	164

SEAFARING SISTERS 166

GEOLOGICAL CALL GIRLS 168

ASHLEY'S FAKE EYELASHES 170

A PIRATEY PROPOSAL 172

FOCUS ON FINISHING 174

THE LUNATIC OF LITERATURE 176

KEEP YOUR HEAD 178

NO CHILD, THANKS TO CROCODILES 180

THE DENTIST OF DEATH 182

ALL OF THE ABOVE 184

SET YOUR SIGHTS ON SUCCESS 186

TRUST YOUR GUT 188

FLIPPING THE BIRD 190

LIFE'S LITTLE CHANGES 192

A MATHEMATICAL MATRIARCH 194

FAME AND FORTUNE 196

SUMMIT FOR YOURSELF 198

HELL IN HEELS 200

PRINCESS PROGRESS   202

TAKE IT BACK   204

CARDIO IS FUCKING HARDIO   206

BORN TO KILL   208

DEEP THOUGHTS, DIRTY LOVERS   210

BOOZY BOTANY   212

LOOK THE PART   214

LAUGHING ALL THE WAY   216

EAT, DRINK, AND THANK EVA   218

HUNG, IN MORE WAYS THAN ONE   220

BEACH TRASH IN PARADISE   222

F*CKING HISTORY

A NO-BULLSHIT BEGINNING

Stories. They educate us, entertain us, and help us relate to others. We've either been told or have told stories our entire lives. Some true, some false. However, regardless of factual accuracy, there's no denying the reality that the right story—delivered at the right time—can give us hope, turning what feels like a bitter end into a situation that we'll someday laugh about with our friends. The right story can motivate us to take a chance. The right story can inspire us to make a change. Or perhaps the right story is simply a story to remind us that life is downright fucking strange. Well, this book is full of stories intended to do all those things. Except, unlike some of the fairy tales and fables that you were told while growing up, these stories aren't works of fiction. These are real stories about real people. As you flip through the following pages, you'll learn about individuals who destroyed kingdoms, people who got exactly what they had coming, and characters who proved just how badass (and bizarre) some humans really are. So whether you're dealing with heartbreak, facing another one of life's headaches, or just looking for a reason to laugh about your mistakes, this book has a story for you.

Going back to the topic of fairy tales, I'm almost positive that everyone reading this is familiar with the story *La Belle et la Bête*. No? What if I told you that's Beauty and the Beast, for all of you barbaric, French-illiterate folk? (Seriously, who raised you?)

Written by the French novelist Gabrielle-Suzanne Barbot de Villeneuve, and published in a collection of her stories in 1740, the tale of love overcoming even the most monstrous of physical and behavioral defects is pretty damn romantic, right? Hmm, not really. You see, Villeneuve's story wasn't a fairy tale. In fact, it was quite the opposite—it was a goddamn nightmare. Because the intention of *La Belle et la*

Bête wasn't to enamor the masses with a story of everlasting love; the purpose of the romance was to groom young girls for the possibility of an arranged marriage, an all-too-common practice for much of the world (and eighteenth-century France was not immune to this type of premarital turmoil).

Now, remember what I said earlier about stories helping us through hard times? Well, I can't think of anything worse than being forced to marry some gross-ass dude you've never met for your family's benefit. And I'd imagine Villeneuve couldn't either, which is why she chose to write a story that (hopefully) made the ordeal feel less terrible. Think of it this way: Your significant other might suck from time to time, but hey, at least you chose to be with them.

Anyway, now that I've destroyed the backstory to one your favorite love stories, allow me to continue doing what I do best for the rest of this book: teaching you some fucking history, full strength and far from watered down. I've combined my two previous titles—along with some new additions—to deliver a veritable collection of valuable life lessons.

Keep in mind, the following stories will be nothing like the ones you heard in school or saw depicted in films by a company that almost rhymes with "kidney." (Personally, I'd rather sell a kidney than be forced into marriage.)

GETTIN' GHOSTED

Few things in life will make you feel as dumb as getting ghosted. But you know what? Getting ghosted is a fucking blessing. Because anybody who won't give you the courtesy of giving it to you straight is somebody you don't need in your life anyway. So if you get ghosted, keep doing your thing and make sure the person who ghosted you lives to absolutely fucking regret it. Be like Edith Wharton.

By the year 1905, Edith had already made quite a name for herself as an author and a wordsmith. Sadly, her literary success did not carry into her marriage. (Apparently, her husband was kind of an angry shithead.) And like unhappily married people have been known to do, she had an affair. It began in 1907 with a kindred spirit and fellow writer by the name of William Morton Fullerton. Edith was head over heels for this guy and thought for sure he was the soul mate most people only dream of meeting. Unfortunately, the affair was short-lived, as Fullerton disappeared on her sometime in 1908. Yep, he straight up ghosted her ass.

Over the years, she did what she could to find him and make contact by writing hundreds of letters—yes, hundreds—in an attempt to get some closure, but Fuckboy Fullerton never bothered to even give her a response. Realizing all her worrying was dumb, Edith gave up and got on with her life. In 1913 she divorced her husband and moved to France. There, she continued to write, and in 1916 she received the French Legion of Honor award for her work during the war. In 1921 she became THE FIRST WOMAN EVER to win a Pulitzer Prize, for her novel *The Age of Innocence*.

As a saucy, scholarly boss, she never remarried and spent the rest of her life writing in the French Riviera, with her dogs, her garden, and her close friends. She even went on to receive three Nobel Prize nominations before her death in 1937. And what did Fullerton do with his life? Not much. His claim to fame was dating Edith, and a selection of the letters she wrote to him were eventually published in a book. Yeah, although he didn't respond, he received *and saved* every single one—all four hundred of 'em. (Huh, suddenly sending five texts in a row doesn't seem so bad.)

You see, getting ghosted is not the end of the world. If someone ghosts you, haunt their ass with your success. Or just get, like, super fucking attractive. Either way, you win, they lose.

TILL DEATH DO YOU PART (OR NOT)

You're a fucking catch. And anyone you date should fucking act like it. Don't waste your time with someone who only wants to hang out at home, doesn't invite you out with their friends, and is an all-around keep-you-to-themselves kind of asshole. Find someone who is proud to be with you and wants to show you off. Like King Pedro (a.k.a. Peter I of Portugal) did with his second wife, Inês de Castro.

Here's his story: After the death of his first wife in 1345 (an arranged marriage), Pedro married Inês against his father's wishes, causing an absolute shitstorm in the royal kingdom. Why? Well, Inês was not of royal blood; thus, their union offered no political advantages. So in 1355, Pedro's father, King Afonso IV, hired three men to kidnap Inês and, well, cut off her fucking head. (And you thought your dad overreacted when you brought your first boyfriend home in high school.)

Upon learning about this, Pedro swore revenge, but he was just a lil' prince without much power. Fortunately for him, he didn't have to wait too long to inherit the power necessary to enact his plan. In 1357, Dad died and Pedro became the new king. And what was King Pedro's first order of business? Simple: He was going to make good on his vengeful promise. He tracked down the three men who'd killed Inês and had their hearts ripped out while they were still alive. Because, as he claimed, they had done the same to him when they killed Inês. (Pretty emo move if you ask me, but I can respect it.)

Then Pedro had Inês's body exhumed, dressed in royal cloth, and seated next to him on a throne as the rightful queen. Yeah, that's how proud Pedro was of her. Dead, without makeup, and with no fucking eyebrows (but probably with some kick-ass skeleton contouring), Pedro still wanted to show her off. So much so that he forced the entire kingdom to form a line, bow, and kiss her dead, bony-ass hands. Now THAT'S a dude who was proud of his relationship and truly didn't give a fuck about what others had to say about it.

(It's worth noting that Pedro went on to become a complete psychopath of a king, known for his affinity for torture, brutality, and living heart removal. But let's not focus on that—let's focus on how proud he was to be married to Inês and how little he cared about the opinions of others.)

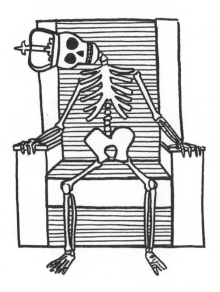

HATERS GONNA HATE

Don't you just hate it when someone asks you to "prove" something? I mean, not only are they calling you a liar; they're also questioning your ability to represent yourself. Essentially, they are insulting you twice. The good news: This kind of scrutiny generally means you're really good at something. And no matter what it is—writing, performing, sports, looking hot—jealous people will always question anything that seems too good to be true. Ever heard of Niccolò Paganini? No? Well, that's too bad. You should probably stop watching reality-TV shows and get some fucking culture in your life, because Niccolò was perhaps the greatest violinist of all time.

Born in northern Italy in 1782, Niccolò developed his musical prowess at a young age, and by 1813 he was regarded by many as the best violinist in European history. He amassed a cult-like following of fans. (I believe these are called "groupies.") He was the first real rock star, both on and, especially, off the stage. But what Paganini did with his private parts is really none of our business, so let's get back to his music and not his manhood.

Niccolò was such a talented musician that a vast majority of folks were convinced he wasn't human; thus, a rumor began to spread that he was actually the son of the devil and his violin contained the soul of a woman he had killed and imprisoned inside. Yeah, pretty fucking ridiculous, but these rumors became so intense and widely believed that in order to continue traveling and performing, Niccolò was forced to prove his humanity by publishing letters and birth documentation from his mother. After proving he wasn't the son of Satan, he was allowed to continue jammin' out—but the belief that he was associated with the devil never really went away, and communal fear continued to affect his career.

Honestly, so what if Niccolò's dad were the devil, as long as Niccolò put on a good show—right? I mean, c'mon, nearly every successful name in music has dabbled in the dark arts at least once in their life. Hell, I've had songs I don't even like stuck in my head for years at time. That's some goddamn witchcraft, if you ask me.

Anyway, the moral of the story: If people doubt you, hate on you, and constantly seem to be out to get you, it usually means you're doing something right—so keep that shit up.

TIMELESS BEAUTY

"Resting bitch face." This term has been floating around a lot the past few years, making its way into a slew of selfies, memes, and pop-culture articles. But it's nothing new. The art of looking like a handsome bitch, dick, or asshole has been around since the beginning of time. Why? Because there's a certain level of respect, mystery, and intrigue that comes from appearing seductive yet absolutely terrifying. For centuries, women have used RBF to lure kings from their thrones, and those kings, in turn, have used RBF to intimidate and conquer rival lands; the history of RBF is firmly rooted in honor, attraction, and self-respect.

And throughout history, self-respect has always been closely related to smiling (or the lack thereof). Aside from the obscenely long exposure times required for old photography to work properly, you don't often see people smiling in old photos or paintings, as it was considered foolish to pose with a smile on your face. Because, well, it was probably fake. To smile for a portrait was not an accurate depiction of emotion. You were smiling just to smile, not because you were genuinely happy. You know, like when you fake a smile for your boss to conceal your complete mental breakdown.

In fact, it was Mark Twain (you know the name) who said, "A photograph is a most important document, and there is nothing more damning to go down to posterity than a silly, foolish smile caught and fixed forever." In my opinion, no truer words have ever been spoken.

Except maybe the infamous TLC line, "Don't go chasing waterfalls." Which, oddly enough, is also a statement concerning self-respect. Huh, weird.

Now, the next time someone asks you why you don't smile in photos, you have some history to school them and validation to support your decision. Tell them you're doing it for your posterity.

TWO'S A COUPLE, THREE'S A CROWD

The ultimate goal of dating: finding your equal. Someone equally as fun, equally as cool, or equally as fucked up as you are. And every now and then you encounter a couple that has successfully done this. These couples give you hope—hope that you too, might someday find a counterpart. Not to mention, people who successfully find their equal are usually "the cool couple." So even your single friends will be happy for you because you'll still be fun to hang out with since you don't have to change who you are to be around your friends and your partner at the same time. This is called acceptance. And no matter how unappealing you think a certain aspect of yourself might be, trust me, there's somebody out there who will accept that odd-ass part of you. Let's discuss this further with a historical example.

In 1860 on the French Caribbean island of Martinique, Blanche Dumas was born with a condition known as tripedalism (three legs), as well as a condition known as uterus didelphys (double sex organs). Which means, you guessed it, two vaginas. (And here you are, worried about your thigh gap with just one. Pfft, you have it easy.) Now you'd think that with her condition, she was doomed to be alone, right? Wrong. Enter Juan Baptista dos Santos from Portugal (born 1843), who—guess what?—also happened to have been born with tripedalism and diphallia (three legs, two dicks). I'm not making this shit up; you can google it, but I don't recommend it.

Anyway, after Blanche and Juan learned about each other through the local freak-show circuit, the two obviously had to meet. Basically, one was peanut butter, the other was jelly, and together they made one hell of a freaky fucking sandwich. It's unknown how long their romance lasted, but it goes to show you, there's somebody out there for everyone.

Stop changing yourself for the people you date, because there really is someone out there who will dig everything about you—even an extra leg. For those of you who have found that person, be glad you met online and not at a local freak show. (Although freak shows tend to have fewer weirdos.)

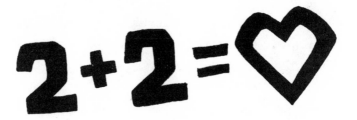

STAGE FRIGHT, DIVORCE FIGHT

If it seems like marriage isn't taken seriously these days, that's because it's not. But during the Middle Ages, marriage was ABSOLUTELY serious shit. When you said "till death do us part," it really meant till fucking death. If you wanted out of a marriage, you pretty much had to wait for your spouse to die—or handle your shit and kill them yourself. Divorce simply wasn't an option.

Plain and simple, if you didn't like the way your husband treated you, you had to poison that fucker's food. I know this sounds morbid, but during this time period, we're talking about a lot of arranged, underage marriages put in place for political reasons, and/or creepy brother-sister marriages set up to maintain the family bloodline. These marriages were hell, and the women were fucking miserable because the Catholic Church simply wouldn't allow for divorce. Basically, your life was over if your uncle's fifty-seven-year-old friend wanted to marry you and your dad decided it would be good for the family.

But this all changed in mid-sixteenth-century France with the introduction of the French impotence courts. Finally women had a way out. If you could prove your husband's dick was as limp as hot spaghetti, the church would grant you a divorce. How would a woman prove this? Easy. She'd bring that freckly old fuck before a judiciary panel, and they'd watch him jerk off—and if he couldn't do it, she was free to begin her new life as a single lady. "Oh my God, look who's single again—you are!"

Let's think about this for a minute though. As a dude, this would totally suck, because "stage fright" is a very real thing. Realizing this, the French added a second part to the impotence proceedings. If the husband—a.k.a. "the owner of the broken dick in question"—wanted help to prove the fact that his junk actually worked, he could request that his wife take part in the act as well. The panel would assume their position, accused husband and angry wife would assume theirs, and that was that. Time to lay some butter on that bread and see who's lying.

So the next time you think the world we live in today is sick and wrong, think about this: At least you can end a marriage without answering the bone phone in front of a judge.

MEOWLESS AND BROWLESS

You think you love your cat? Wrong. You might "like" your cat, but you definitely don't love him or her—at least not as much as the ancient Egyptians loved their felines. Seriously, the Egyptians fucking LOVED cats. They liked dogs too, but cats were the real deal. Egyptians adorned their cats with jewels, fed them as if they were royalty, and treated them better than they did most people—like you probably do, because a lot of people suck.

Personally, I think cats are fucking weird; they freak me out. When a cat looks at you, it could be thinking about cuddling up under your arm or eating your face while you sleep. That's how unpredictable they are. And that unpredictability is probably what made the Egyptians love them so much, because the ancient Egyptians themselves were fucking psychos. But Egyptian torture techniques are a topic for another day—back to the kitty cats . . . Okay, maybe just one: The Egyptians used to strip people naked, cover them in milk and honey, tie them between two boats floating in stagnant water, and simply leave. Use your imagination. (HINT: Lots of hungry-ass bugs live around stagnant water, and hungry-ass bugs love milk, honey, and holes— almost as much as the Egyptians loved their cats.)

Obviously, when a cat died, the Egyptians were fucking devastated. And they chose to mourn their loss very publicly. First, they would shave off their eyebrows to symbolize the loss of their furry pet. When the meows go, the brows go. That's just the Egyptian way. The cat was then mummified and placed in the family tomb. The grieving period lasted until your eyebrows grew back. (Which takes fucking FOR-EVER, by the way.)

Damn, the Egyptians make your weak-ass social media posts about how much you love your pet look pretty lame. All I'm trying to say is this: If you really love your cat, you'll shave off your eyebrows when the unfortunate day comes. I mean, it's not like I'm suggesting anything too crazy—you already look like you don't have eyebrows when you take off your makeup anyway.

A CATFISH CRUSADE

"Catfishing" is nothing new. Sure, the internet made it easier, online dating made it extremely prevalent, and some network even made it a TV show, but catfishing has been around for thousands of years. To prove it, let's go back to a time when two major forces, the Persians and the Egyptians, ruled much of the civilized world.

In an effort to keep peace between the two kingdoms, the Persian emperor Cambyses II asked Pharaoh Amasis II to arrange his marriage to the pharaoh's daughter. But Amasis knew that if he did this, his daughter would be treated as simply another notch in Cambyses's belt, rather than an actual wife. Cambyses didn't exactly have a reputation as a respectful dude. In fact, he was known as quite the womanizing douche. So Amasis sent a pharaoh's daughter—just not his daughter. Instead, he sent the daughter of his predecessor, the deceased Pharaoh Apries. Thus the first recorded catfish in history was underway. The year was approximately 526 BC. (You see, catfishing has been around for-fucking-ever.)

When Cambyses realized he'd been deceived, he was furious and immediately declared war on the Egyptian kingdom. Now, things didn't exactly happen as quickly back then as they do today, so by the time Cambyses had gathered his forces and made the trek to Egypt, Pharaoh Amasis was already dead. It was now the duty of Amasis's son, Pharaoh Psamtik III, to defend against Cambyses's Catfish Crusade of 525 BC—otherwise known as the Battle of Pelusium.

So, just how does one go about seeking revenge after being catfished? Well, with a catfight, of course. No, really. The reason Cambyses took so long to organize his retaliation was that he needed to collect a shitload of cats. He knew that the Egyptians worshipped cats (we just discussed this), so Cambyses had his army use cats as shields. His men literally marched into battle carrying cats. And fearful of harming the very animals that represented their goddess Bastet, the Egyptians refused to fire arrows or throw spears at the Persian invaders. Which, of course, led to an absolute fucking slaughter and decisive Persian victory. (Seriously, why are cat people so fucking weird?)

Now, after you text your friend about the history lesson you just learned, get off your phone. For real, stop using your phone—or your cat—as a shield to avoid human interaction. Go the fuck outside.

KIS(S)MET

Expectations set the tone of every situation. Sometimes our expectations work in our favor; other times our expectations leave us wishing it would all be over—particularly when our expectations lead to heartbreak. Nobody likes to be led on. And most of us (I can't speak for everyone, because some of you are sick fucks) don't like leading others on, because it feels wrong. But what if the other person deserves it? I mean, what if leading someone on can actually be beneficial to everyone (except the person being led on, of course)? Perhaps you could teach them a lesson, leave a lasting impression, or simply prevent others from falling victim to the person's less-than-noble behavior. Would you do it then? Still no? Well, let me share a story that will make you change your mind. Occasionally it's totally okay to mess with somebody's feelings.

In 1940, after their anti-Nazi protests had caught the attention of a local commander, sisters Freddie and Truus Oversteegen joined the Dutch urban resistance against Nazi Germany—with the permission of their mother, of course. At the time, Freddie was only fourteen, and Truus was only sixteen. The outspoken and spirited siblings, along with twenty-year-old Hannie Schaft, were taught to shoot, trained in the art of sabotage, and encouraged to use their God-given gifts of feminine flirtation to fight against the Nazis and any of their dipshit supporters.

Together, the trio sheltered victims who were fleeing oppression, organized and executed drive-by shootings on their bicycles (okay, that's badass), and, most notably, hung out at the local bars. But it was what they did after leaving these bars that was the real act of heroism. You see, Freddie, Truus, and Hannie would lure drunk, dumb, and deserving Nazi jackasses (and their friends) into the woods with the promise of some good kissing—and later, these horny hopefuls would "mysteriously" go missing.

Essentially, the girls would ask them to "take a stroll" in the forest, where the only thing their drool-covered lips would be kissing was a hot bullet. The trio never revealed how many Nazis and known supporters they killed this way because, according to Freddie, "Soldiers don't say." (Also, killing was not something they were proud of, but it was something they knew had to be done.) Unfortunately, only a few weeks before the war ended, Hannie was arrested by the Gestapo and sentenced to death in 1945. Thankfully, the sisters lived to tell the tale of their bravery and necessary late-night trickery, each living to the age of ninety-two. (Truus died in 2016; Freddie, in 2018.)

Now, I don't condone the act of leading someone on—unless you find yourself meeting a lot of Nazis. In that case, you might want to reconsider the dating sites you're using.

APPLE ALLURE

Okay, there's no point in beating around the bushel, so we're going to get right into this one. Back in nineteenth-century Austria, women used to place an apple slice in their armpit before taking to the dance floor. (Why the armpit? Well, because it's within easy reach, and also because a dress with pockets looks fucking homely.) The lady would keep her apple slice warm as she danced the night away with a multitude of male suitors. When the music stopped and the night was over, she'd present her sweaty pit fruit to whichever man she was interested in further pursuing. This is where it gets really fucking weird, because if the guy shared her interest, he'd eat her salty slice, thus signifying he was into her.

Now I don't know about you, but I would never eat someone's hot fruit on a first date—that's some third-, fourth-, or maybe even fifth-date kind of shit. However, I do respect the talent it must have required to keep an apple slice from falling out of your armpit while you twerk the night away. Hell, these women might as well have put some flour and an egg in their armpit along with that apple—while they heated things up on the dance floor, their body could have heated up an apple pie. "Impressive multitasking, Elizabeth."

We can actually learn a lot from this apple tradition; it might even be worth bringing back. Like my grandma always said, "The fastest way to a man's heart is through his stomach." I mean, not only is this technique a great way to offer the hungry drunk guy a snack after he's finished dry-humping your leg, it's clearly an even better way to gauge his level of interest in you. Because if a dude is willing to eat something you made with your own sweat and body heat, he really likes you—maybe even like likes you . . . keep your fingers crossed.

So the next time you go out with your girls, leave your purse in the car. Your body has all the curves and snack pockets you need.

SQUAD GOALS

A girl squad is like a flock of birds: If you spook one, you spook 'em all. And if you're dating one of them, you're pretty much dating all of them. Because every fight, every photo, every text—EVERYTHING you do (or do not do)—will become subject to the squad's ridicule, investigation, and approval. But it's not all bad. If you're a decent guy, your girlfriend's squad might actually be your greatest asset. If they like you, your girlfriend's friends will be your strongest advocates during those times when your girlfriend is about to lose her fucking mind. Women trust the shit out of their friends, and that's why squads exist. Even great queens throughout history have relied on their squad to approve of potential suitors. Don't believe me?

Catherine the Great ruled Russia from 1762 until 1796, making her the longest-running female leader in Russia's history. She was smart, savvy, sophisticated, and goddamn fierce. Under her rule and military command, Russia was established as a dominant power. (You're welcome, Russia—a lady did that. Now cheer the fuck up.) Anyway, you'd think a woman as mighty and smart as Catherine wouldn't need girlfriends for advice, right? Wrong. Catherine was a sex fiend. She was rich, she was powerful, and she liked a mouthful. I'm talking some real *Game of Thrones* type of shit; you can see what I'm saying by googling "Catherine the Great's dick chair."

Obviously, due to her position and reputation, she couldn't go around fucking just anybody—she was the empress of Russia, for God's sake. So she enlisted the help of her squad. In order to get to Catherine, you had to go through them. Literally. If Catherine thought you were hot, she'd ask you to sleep with a member of her court first to make sure you were able to satisfy her own royal thirst. If you came up short, it was mission abort, and Catherine was on to the next one. (Damn, at least with a dick pic you get a few moments to explain yourself.)

Now, guys, I know it's occasionally a pain in the ass, but learn to play nice with your girlfriend's friends; you never know when you might need them on your side. Yes, even Ashley. (I know, I don't get it either. Ashley's a fucking mess. Nobody should be taking advice from her.)

TOO MANY TO NAME

So, just how many dogs is too many? Three? Four? FIVE? For the sake of time, let's settle on five. I mean, sure, by today's standards that's a lot of dogs to own. But when we look back through history, that's nothing compared with the number of dogs owned by Kublai Khan.

However, before we talk about his pups, I want you to learn more about who Kublai Khan was.

From May 5, 1260, to February 18, 1294, Kublai Khan was the supreme khan of the Mongols, the first emperor of the Yuan dynasty, AND the emperor of China.

(Pretty impressive résumé.) Essentially, he was the fucking man. So what does the fucking man do? Well, he owns a lot of fucking dogs. How many? Five thousand. Yeah, you read that right: Khan owned FIVE THOUSAND mastiffs. Seriously, take a moment to imagine what a pack of five thousand dogs looks like . . . I don't know how you're picturing it, but I imagine that looking at a pack of five thousand dogs is a lot like looking at a bathtub filled with five thousand bags of M&M's: You know it's a bad idea, but for some reason, you still want 'em all.

Now, if Khan had owned five thousand cats, it wouldn't have been nearly as impressive or intimidating. It would have completely changed the way his rivals viewed him. Instead of looking like a badass, he'd look like a crazy, lonely weirdo. Basically, what I'm saying is, if you know you're doomed to be single your entire life, don't banish yourself to the life of "the crazy cat neighbor." Instead, be a damn cool dog owner. With a lot of dogs, people won't even feel sorry for you. They'll just be like, "Damn, what a badass." And instead of looking like you belong on one of those TV shows about hoarding, you'll look like someone who's anything but boring.

What are you waiting for? Go fill the backseat of your car with beef jerky, drive slowly around town with the doors open, and start collecting strays—because it's going to take you a while to get to five thousand and become Kublai Khan kind of cool.

SETTLING IS A SLOW DEATH

When you settle, you not only set yourself back, you also set back those around you. Settling is accepting instead of attempting. And I'm not just talking about settling in a relationship sense; I'm talking about settling for doing less than what you're capable of accomplishing each day, settling for saying less than what you know you should say, or settling for tortilla chips instead of ordering an entrée. My point is, we settle for less nearly every fucking day. And if it becomes a habit, it becomes a problem—settling creates comfort, and comfort creates nothing. That's why we need people like Maud Gonne to remind us that settling is for suckers.

In 1866, Maud was born in England. Her mother died young, and Maud was sent to boarding school to receive an education. After graduation, she traveled with her dad (an army guy) to Dublin. In 1886, he died, and Maud made the move to France. Here, she met/dated Lucien Millevoye, sparking her interest in activism and spurring her decision to return to Dublin. Over the next several decades, in addition to being a fashion icon—google her, and if you don't agree, you can fight me—Maud started a revolution, established a newspaper, and even had a stint as a stage actress. On top of all this, she had a love life better than that shown on any daytime television show: three children, two baby daddies, five marriage proposals (four from the same dude), one divorce, AND coffin sex—yeah, she did it all. It's worth mentioning that the dude who proposed to her four times was the famous Irish poet W. B. Yeats; however, Maud, in true muse fashion, rejected him constantly so he'd have sad-ass shit to write poems about. She actually said, "The world should thank me for not marrying you."

In 1918, she was arrested and served six months in jail for her political activism. In 1922, she was arrested for leading the Women's Peace Committee and the

Women's Prisoner Defence League. In 1923, she was arrested for creating antigovernment signs and literature. And she continued with her non-settling, selective-fuck-giving life until 1953, dying at the age of eighty-six. However, her attitude was clearly passed down to her son, Seán MacBride, who was awarded a Nobel Peace Prize in 1974.

So in remembrance of Maud, if you're ever tempted to settle for the sake of ease or comfort, remember that truly living will always come with some trouble and effort.

THE STRAP OF WRATH

Nothing is permanent. With time, everything can change. The silly shit that stressed you out five years ago is no longer important. That breakup you thought would be the end of you quickly became old news. And that embarrassing video from last weekend's shenanigans will soon be forgotten (give it a few weeks). The more power you give a moment in time, the longer it will haunt you.

In 1884, French art lovers came in droves to see John Singer Sargent's latest masterpiece, because the subject of this particular painting was just as popular as Sargent himself: Sargent had asked the beautiful Amélie Gautreau to pose for him. In her early twenties at the time, Amélie was a well-known socialite and Parisian fashion icon. So naturally her reputation (as well as Sargent's) was riding on the release of this freshly finished canvas titled *Portrait de Mme ****. The debut was a fucking disaster. The painting was met with ridicule and repulsion, leaving both parties horrified and humiliated. Basically, everybody thought Amélie looked trashy because her dress strap was hanging off her shoulder. Who would have thought a little black dress could cause so much distress? "Oh my God, Becky—lookest at her strap." (That's an old-timey remix of Sir Mix-a-Lot, which was surprisingly popular in nineteenth-century France.)

Attempting some quick reputation repair, Sargent repainted and repositioned the salacious strap, but it was too late—Amélie felt destroyed and went into hiding, effectively retiring from society. She lived the remainder of her life as a hermitess, going so far as to remove all the mirrors in her home. In 1915, she died in obscurity, one year before her beauty would receive worldwide recognition when the now renamed *Portrait of Madame X* was purchased by the Metropolitan Museum of Art in New York City. Regarded as Sargent's greatest artwork, this portrait served as fashion inspiration for many designers of the early 1900s, making Amélie's once trashy gown the talk of the town—sucks that she wasn't around to see it.

Anyway, the next time you don't think you'll get over something, don't stress out, put on your best strappy dress, and go out. Live your fucking life, and don't let a single moment define you.

PIGGYBACKS SAVE LIVES

You haven't truly lived until you've given a really drunk person a piggyback ride. Especially if you're equally as drunk yourself. Because nothing will bring you closer as friends or strengthen your relationship more than stumbling around city streets together like conjoined, drunk idiots—too dumb to request a car, too drunk to give a fuck. Seriously, a good piggyback can be a lifesaver, both figuratively and literally. Figuratively in the sense that you don't want to scuff the new Louboutins you just spent half your paycheck on; and literally as in what the men of Weinsberg, Germany, experienced during King Conrad III's siege on their castle.

You see, King Conrad was not a patient man, and on one particular day in 1140, he'd grown tired of his failed attempts to take Weinsberg Castle. So rather than continue fighting and failing, he offered the castle inhabitants a deal: Stop resisting and he'd allow all the women to go free, along with whatever valuables they could carry on their backs. As for the men, they were fucked. He would behead them all. Well, as any man should do in order to protect his wife, all the men agreed to the deal and stopped fighting— sacrificing themselves and accepting their fate as dead men. (To their wives, I like to imagine they all looked like Channing Tatum during this moment: just super noble and handsome.)

Now here's where the story gets good. Adhering to

the king's offer, the women loaded up their backs with their most-prized possessions: their husbands. I'm sure a few women opted to leave theirs behind, but for the most part, each woman carried her man out of the castle—piggybacking them to safety. Damn, those are some tough chicks. They didn't even have CrossFit back then. Anyway, when the king's troops saw what was happening, they were fucking furious. But King Conrad was quite amused with the cleverness the women showed. So he replied to his troops, "A king should always stand by his word." And he did, allowing all the men and women of Weinsberg Castle to live.

After this event, the women of Weinsberg became known as Treue Weiber, meaning "loyal women." And the castle grounds were later renamed Weibertreu.

Well, there you have it, dudes. Treat your ladies right. You never know when you might need her to carry your dumb ass to safety. Or at least help you onto the couch when you've had too much to drink.

TEMPER TANTRUMS

Now, there's overreacting, and then there's OVER-FUCKING-REACTING. You all know what I'm talking about. "Overreacting" can simply be defined as "going too far." For girls, it's the difference between telling your boyfriend to fuck off and using scissors to actually cut the words "fuck" and "off" into all his favorite T-shirts. (Funny, but depending on what he actually did, you might be going too far.) For guys, it's the difference between being slightly annoyed that your girlfriend still talks to her ex and telling her that if she doesn't delete her account or block him immediately, you're done. Relax, dude. In the age of the internet and social media, nobody is able to completely disconnect from an ex unless they move to North Korea or go to prison. Just accept the fact that you're not the only guy on the planet and stop acting like a petty dumbass.

Basically, don't be like Ibrahim "the Mad." You see, Ibrahim I was sultan of the Ottoman Empire from 1640 to 1648, and was quite the womanizer. And like most womanizers, he was extremely insecure and quick-tempered, and required the constant validation of new females—evident with his obscenely large harem of 280 women. So, what does this story have to do with overreacting? Well, I'm about to tell you.

When one of Ibrahim's concubines decided to sleep with someone other than Ibrahim (probably a handsome, cool dude like your girlfriend's ex), Ibrahim "the Insecure" lost his fucking shit. He threw a tantrum like no other and had 278 (some sources say all 280) of his concubines bound with rope and drowned in the Bosporus Strait as punishment for the one disobeying him and the others protecting her. That's pretty much the historical equivalent of forcing your girlfriend to delete her social media accounts. Because, let's be honest, without social media, you might as well be dead.

Cool, you just learned some history. You also learned that Ibrahim was a fucking dick. So yeah, don't be that guy.

REINVENTING YOURSELF

Shit happens—relationships end, jobs are lost, and, well, life doesn't always go the way you'd planned. Maybe you were a supercute kid growing up and thought for sure you were destined for a career in modeling, but the blooming teenage years were harsh. (Let's just say you emerged looking more like a caterpillar and less like a butterfly.) That's life. Sometimes things happen that force you to look at your alternatives in order to continue moving forward. And THAT is fucking great. It's an opportunity to reinvent yourself and become even cooler than you were before.

Going back to the example of the formerly cute kid turned high school hunchback: If life deals you a caterpillar face, use those bug eyes to your advantage. You could easily become an actor—one who makes tons of money playing a creepy stalker, a praying mantis, or a serial killer. My point is, with an open mind, it's never "the end." Take, for example, King Eric VII of Denmark, also known as Eric of Pomerania or Erik av Pommern. (Yeah, lots of alternative spellings here.)

You see, Eric was the king of Denmark from 1389 to 1442, the king of Sweden from 1396 to 1439, and also the king of Norway from 1396 to 1439. (Quite the curriculum vitae.) Unfortunately, despite his being a charming and charismatic leader, a series of public rebellions began during the 1430s. So in 1439, Eric simply said, "Fuck you, dorks—I'm out." Fed up with the rebellions, he went on strike and moved into his secluded Castle Visborg on the island of Gotland. (Kind of like Elsa's ice palace.)

When it became clear he was in no hurry to come back, the nobles of the countries he'd left behind called his bluff and deposed him as their king—not exactly the idea Eric had in mind. But he wasn't the kind of guy who easily gave up. So he took advantage of his leadership experience to reinvent himself as the perfect pirate. And for the next ten years, he kidnapped ships, held ports for ransom, and did all sorts of piratey things in order to maintain his lavish lifestyle and once again say, "Fuck you," to his former countrymen. Talk about taking control of your life. Bravo, Eric—bra-fucking-vo.

I want you to remember this story the next time life gets shitty or something doesn't go as planned. Use it as an opportunity to become something better—and despite what your teachers told you when you were growing up, YOU CAN become a fucking pirate.

INFLUENCED BY AFFLUENCE

It's both a blessing and a curse to live in a world so technologically immersed. Every day we take advantage of on-demand transportation, easier-than-ever communication, and, well, technology that gives us the ability to share every damn second of our day—whether it's worth documenting or not (generally the latter).

It's all too easy, which unfortunately has removed much of life's mystery. Before every phone was equipped with a camera, you had to be selective about what was actually worthy of photographic permanence. You had to painstakingly fucking paint your selfies—unless you were rich. With enough money, you could hire somebody else to paint them for you, which is exactly what Marie de' Medici did in 1621. As the queen of France, wife of Henry IV, and descendant of the House of Medici, Marie had enough status, wealth, and fame to last a dozen lifetimes, but what she didn't have was a way of effectively telling the story of her extraordinary life. So at the age of forty-six (prime time for a midlife crisis), she commissioned the highly sought-after artist Peter Paul Rubens to paint a series of twenty-one paintings to explain her life—from infancy to regency (plus three extra portraits of herself and her parents).

And to ensure the stories of her grandiose existence were depicted properly, each of these paintings had to be fucking huge (about four meters in height). Rubens accepted the job as Marie's "Instagram husband," and they began working together to showcase the most impressive moments of Marie's life. Over the span of two years, they portrayed her childhood struggles, her fearless involvement in the military, her powerful command of exploration, and everything else that made Marie a badass queen worth remembering. Essentially, Marie's life was fucking wild, and now she had the paintings to prove it.

Except there was one problem: The stories were bullshit. They were complete exaggerations and false interpretations of her luxurious yet largely uneventful reign. Marie simply had the means to fake the life of her dreams. Essentially, she was the original influencer, and her "influence," known as the "Marie de' Medici Cycle," is currently displayed at the Louvre in Paris (at least during the time I'm writing this), but influencers delete shit all the time, so these paintings could be gone at any moment.

A TRULY LOYAL ROYAL

Popular culture has given us a lot of bullshit over the past few years: cinnamon-flavored whiskey, pumpkin-spice everything, and the general notion that "hoes ain't loyal." I get it, that was a catchy song, but—if you're reading this, and you're a guy—it's time you move on from that mind-set. Trust me, there are still some women like Olga of Kiev out there. You just have to be worthy and ready to actually date one.

Olga was a princess during the tenth century in an area now divided between Ukraine and Russia. And like most women from that region, she was absolutely fucking gorgeous. She was also extremely loyal to her family, her country, and her man. So naturally, tons of dudes wanted her. So much so that the jealousy of other men eventually led to the assassination of her husband, Igor of Kiev, who was killed by the rival Drevlians, who hoped to convince Olga to marry one of their own, Prince Mal. But Olga didn't want anything to do with their Drevlian bullshit. She had her man, she lost her man, and her son was now the only man who mattered in her life. She would rather die—sad, wrinkly, alone, and smothered in fucking cats—than ever marry Prince Mal's Drevlian ass.

So when Mal sent twenty of his finest negotiators in an attempt to persuade Olga to accept his marriage proposal, she had all twenty of them buried alive. When he sent a group of nobles as a follow-up, Olga had them locked in a bathhouse and burned alive. Olga then pretended to apologize by inviting all the Drevlians to a party. At that party, she had her army kill five thousand men—but she wasn't done yet. Olga then invaded the Drevlians' lands and had her army burn down every fucking house. (In case you haven't caught on, Olga really liked fire.) I think it was about this time that Prince Mal realized Olga was too much woman for him and gave up trying to pursue her.

Olga continued to rule over Kievan Rus' as a single, independent woman from 945 to 963 on behalf of her son, until he was old enough to rule alone.

Now, ladies, if a guy ever questions your loyalty or calls you a "ho," be like Olga and burn his fucking house down.

FEAR OF MISSING OUT

FOMO. For those of you who didn't read the title of this lesson, that's short for "fear of missing out." FOMO can apply to nearly every aspect of life. Unfortunately, with jobs, family, and other responsibilities, you'll never be able to experience everything; you're going to miss out—often. That's just part of being a functioning adult. But you know what? It's not that bad. Sure, it can be frustrating, but not nearly as frustrating as what happened to former horse trainer turned jockey Frank Hayes.

You think missing last Friday's party was bad? Well, this poor bastard missed out on the biggest moment in his racing career. He won, but he wasn't there to enjoy it. How does that fucking happen? I'll tell you. On June 4, 1923, Frank suffered a fatal heart attack midway through a race at New York's Belmont Park. He died, but his horse kept running and actually won the fucking race. The weirdest part: Nobody even noticed Frank was dead until afterward. The officials went over to congratulate him on his first-ever career win and found a corpse saddled in. Frank's dead, lifeless body was just bobbing around on top while the horse did all the work. (You know, like a terrible sexual partner—physically they're there, but other than that, they're fucking lifeless.) Talk about missing out: The greatest accomplishment of Frank's life and he wasn't even there to enjoy it. Hopefully, somebody in heaven threw him a celebration party.

Anyway, FOMO sucks, but as long as you're there for the big, important moments of your life—like winning your first race—it's okay to miss a party here and there. Prioritize, and pray that you don't die when something really cool actually happens.

Well, now that you've learned something new, you should go out and experience something new. Sign up for a pottery class or some shit. You wouldn't want to miss out on the opportunity to make a cool mug or something, would you?

FAKE IT, SEE HOW THEY TAKE IT

We all know what it's like to try to interpret someone's body language, analyze their subtle cues, and read between the lines of each and every text message. Why do we do this? Because we want to know if they feel the same way about us as we do about them. Do they like me? Do they really like me? Plain and simple, dating is confusing. And now, with social media, texting, dating apps, and a variety of other confusing modern-day creations, the relationship Rubik's Cube is harder to solve than ever before.

Sure, you can spend your time googling lists and articles about how to tell if a guy or girl likes you. Personally, I like what Lord Timothy Dexter did to shake up the New England socialite society of the eighteenth century: He faked his own death. Not a big deal; well, until you consider he was married at the time AND attended his own funeral as one of the nearly three thousand guests. (Attending my own funeral

IT'S A TEST

is definitely on my bucket list.) But out of those thousands in attendance, Mr. Dexter was really only concerned about the reaction of one individual in particular: his wife, Mrs. Dexter.

Anyway, guess what? She didn't even cry at the funeral. WHAT THE FUCK? So the not-so-dead Timothy was forced to reveal himself. After confronting Mrs. Dexter about her lack of emotion, he proceeded to publicly cane her. Which is pretty fucked up because it's exactly what it sounds like. I mean, I would have just told her it was over and I was taking the dogs (maybe even the kids), but Tim had a bit of a temper. Not too surprising—it takes someone pretty unstable to fake their own death.

However, what he did was actually kind of brilliant. It's a great way to tell if somebody shares the same level of devotion that you do. So the next time you have questions about the seriousness of your relationship, don't eliminate faking your death as an option. It's fucked up, but it's effective.

SUPPORT YOURSELF

Here's a little fact you probably didn't know about boob control: That elastic-clasp bra strap you've been taking for granted all these years was invented by none other than the famous author Samuel L. Clemens.

After filing for a patent in 1871, Clemens was more than ecstatic—and far from humble—about his incredible elastic creation. How do we know this? Well, because he wrote the following phrase on the patent application: "The advantages of such an adjustable and detachable elastic strap are so obvious that they need no explanation." He claimed the invention was useful for vests, pants, and any other garment requiring adjustment. Fortunately, the "other garment" category really took off. Thank God, right? That's the category that needed Clemens's creation the most.

As a girl, could you imagine trying to control your sweater puppies without this device? As a guy, well, you can thank Samuel for helping you easily let the dogs out. (And dudes, don't act like you're fucking smooth. I guarantee you've been so excited and shaky—trembling like a Chihuahua about to take a piss—that you've considered using scissors. "Oh my God, I'm gonna see a nipple.")

Anyway, before this device, women had the choice of either wrapping up like a mummy, forcing their girls into a corset, or simply saying "Fuck it" and walking around flapping like the ears of a bloodhound. (Are you getting tired of my dog references yet? Good, because I'm not either.) I guess all I'm trying to say is, long before Victoria had a secret, Samuel Clemens had a vision.

Oh, and did I mention Clemens's pen name was Mark Twain?

Yeah, THE Mark Twain. The same dude who wrote that book about Tom and Huck not giving a fuck and running away to an island. You also read about him earlier in this book—and, yes, even Mark Twain smiled when he saw some puppies. Anyway, take it easy and don't let the dogs out. (Unless I'm invited.)

SHOW SOME RESPECT

Moving on to another story about boobs: Let's be honest, everybody loves them. I mean, except for some absolute prudes, everyone enjoys a good set of boobs.

Seriously, girls like their own boobs, guys like their girl's boobs, and girls like other girls' boobs—even gay men appreciate them. So I'll say it again: "EVERYBODY LOVES BOOBS." Now there's obviously a debate in regard to size, shape, real, fake, and a bunch of other shit I don't really want to get into right now. Regardless of your natural or procedural preference, boobs deserve your respect. In other words, if they aren't your boobs, don't be fucking touching them.

Take, for example, the French physician René Théophile Hyacinthe Laennec. Not only was Laennec the inventor of the original stethoscope; he was also a fucking professional and exemplary boob respecter. In 1816, Laennec didn't feel right putting his head up against a female patient's chest in order to examine her heart rhythm. (Why? Because he was fucking respectful, that's why.) So he improvised and quickly fashioned together a sturdy tube consisting of several sheets of rolled paper. And it worked. He could hear the beautiful rhythm of the patient's heart perfectly.

Laennec continued to improve on his design, and the first documented use of his stethoscope was March 8,

1817. Oh, and he came up with the name "stethoscope"—Greek for "I see the chest"—after getting tired of all the stupid names his friends were calling his invention.

Eventually, decades of innovation led to the prop we now see used by unqualified nurses and well-endowed doctors in today's medical-themed pornos. Congratulations, Laennec. Your device has truly come full circle.

Well, you just learned something new. You're welcome. Now remember: It's okay to look—everybody does—but don't you dare touch them without permission, you pervs.

FROM THE THEATRE
TO THE THRONE

.

What you do for work does not determine your personal worth. If you're working a job you hate, a job you're embarrassed by, or maybe a job that leaves you feeling overqualified, take comfort in knowing that by no fucking means does your current place in life determine your absolute place in life. For example, there's Empress Theodora of Byzantium.

From farm girl to one of the most powerful women of the Old World, Theodora is the very definition of defying your background and previous profession. So how did she become so goddamn great? Well, let's investigate. (No, not a creepy, let's-stalk-her-Instagram type of investigation. We're going to use actual fucking history, not modern-day dating strategy.)

Born sometime around AD 500, Theodora was of humble roots: Her father was an animal keeper and she was one of three daughters. Times were hard. Her father died young, and in an effort to improve the family's financial situation, Theodora and her sisters became stage actresses. However, as struggling actresses, they were led to a more lucrative career: prostitution. But Theodora didn't let this get the best of her. She made connections, owned her situation, and got her acting career back on track.

Then, as a respected thespian, she met Justinian, heir to the Byzantine throne. He saw her as his intellectual equal, and she soon became his lover and trusted adviser. The two were married in 523. In 527, Justinian assumed his royal role, and Theodora became the empress. She spearheaded legal reform that banned forced prostitution—but ensured that all the women were provided with other means of financially supporting themselves instead of being left in the streets. Furthermore, she awarded women parental rights, property rights, inheritance rights, and, best of all, divorce rights—"Later, loser." All in all, she was an absolute political force to be reckoned with until her death from illness in 548.

The next time you're feeling frustrated and stuck, remember this: Theodora went from shaking her butt to running an empire. Everything can be an opportunity when you apply the right amount of tenacity.

CROWN ON, CLAWS OUT

In life, people are going to try to take what's yours. You can't avoid this, but you can make taking something so damn difficult that few people are willing to even try. Promotions, lovers, or leftovers—nothing is safe. Because coworkers, hoes, bros, and roommates will come for what's yours like it's already theirs.

So let's learn from one of the best about how to maintain your fucking reign and keep others from taking your fucking things. Born in 1160, Tamar was the daughter of George III, king of Georgia. With a dead wife and no sons, George knew that his nephew would someday take his kingdom. To avoid this, he crowned Tamar "co-ruler" when she was eighteen. In 1184, George died, and Tamar assumed the throne as queen regnant, a.k.a. a queen without a king. Essentially, Tamar was more powerful than a traditional king because she didn't have to share anything. (Think of this as being rich AND single.) This level of womanly supremacy was not what the Georgian aristocrats wanted, and many of them began to devise her demise. She tortured some, had others fired, and quickly established herself as a lady not to be taken lightly. The next attempt to unseat her was to require her to marry some loser named Yuri. In retaliation, Tamar declared herself "Queen of Kings" and didn't allow King Yuri to do a damn thing. He failed at seizing the throne, and in 1187 Tamar defied the church and divorced him. To showcase her power, she later had him banished from the country entirely. "Boy, bye."

Then, realizing it might be wise to have a bloodline, she chose a new husband: David, a military commander and prince from the kingdom of Alania. However, Tamar didn't make him a king; she gave him the title "king consort," which basically meant his job was to serve and support her. For the next twenty-five years, King Tamar (as she liked to be called) led Georgia into its most profitable and powerful stage, ushering in a golden age. She was loved by the people and referred to as "one with the skin of a tiger." Sadly, unlike a cat, she didn't have nine lives and died in 1213; her power passed down to her son and daughter.

Now, if you're like me, this badass woman's story makes you kind of horny—leading seamlessly into the next two pages and a story that will likely leave you both confused and hungry.

CAN'T TOUCH THIS

Sometimes the sweetest things in life come from sinister beginnings. Not everything (or everyone) began as what you see and know today. An enjoyable personality or a particularly delicious dish is often the result of someone's misfortune or failed experiment. And, well, graham crackers are the perfect example of this shit.

Here's the deal: The crackers you've grown to associate with s'mores, piecrusts, and a multitude of dipping uses were created by the Presbyterian minister Sylvester Graham in 1829 as part of "the Graham Diet." So what was up with Graham's churchy-ass cracker diet? Well, Graham believed his crackers would stop someone from masturbating, also known as "using their imagination"—something we encourage all kids to do. (Talk about sending mixed signals.) Pastor Graham preached that clean, untainted food supports a clean, untainted mind. Thus suppressing the urge to butter your own biscuit. It's important to note that the original recipe for graham crackers was basically just flour and water—pretty bland stuff. (Like missionary position with the lights off.)

Why did Pastor Graham hate people using their imaginations so much? I have no idea—probably something he read in an old book. Anyway, if you were caught playing patty-cake with your privates as a teenager, you'd be put on a diet regimen of graham crackers, vegetables, fresh milk, and eggs. No spices, no sweeteners, and definitely no happiness. It was pretty much the food equivalent of dry humping in a blanket fort.

I don't know about you, but as a teenager, I would have needed a hell of a lot more than some boring crackers to keep me from crumbling my own bread. Something like a glove covered in thumbtacks, or anything slightly resembling a garbage dis-posal. But even then I'd probably risk it if I started thinking too much about those old-timey corsets.

Needless to say, Graham was a fucking square (must be how he got the idea for the shape of his crackers). However, his flavorless beliefs did encourage a man by the name of John Harvey Kellogg to continue the promotion of bland food and boring thoughts. (No wonder I hated corn flakes growing up.)

Anyway, whether you like cereal or not, I felt this story was interesting food for thought. Try not to think about it the next time you touch yourself.

HE(A)DY TIMES IN HOLLYWOOD

Some people are simply rogues. They can't be changed, they can't be explained, and they sure as hell can't be tamed. What others consider crazy, they consider a lifestyle. What others disapprove of, they take inspiration from. And what others see as fearful, they see as fun-filled. It's these fun-loving, risk-taking, crazy fucking weirdos who create the most change and make life more interesting. If you could choose only one friend to help you organize an uprising, would you ask your quiet, polite friend—or your foulmouthed, outspoken, sarcastic-ass one? Exactly. You need a friend like Hedy Lamarr.

Hedy was not only a successful Hollywood actress, but she was also an inventor, a producer, and an all-around badass. (She was also married six times, which brings us back to the first two sentences of this lesson. In fact, she once said, "I must quit marrying men who feel inferior to me. I need a superior inferior man.") You see, Hedy was more than a pretty face; she was an acquired taste—the kind of person who is either hated or loved but never ignored.

An Austrian by birth, Hedy made her big-screen debut in 1933 with a controversial role in the Czech film *Ecstasy*. Shortly after, she made some Hollywood connections and spent the next twenty years crushing movie roles as often as she did new husbands. In between movie and dude domination, Hedy was an inventor whose IQ became just as famous as her eyebrows—with one of her most popular quotes being "Any girl can be glamorous. All you have to do is stand still and look stupid."

In 1941, Hedy worked with spread-spectrum radio frequency to help codevelop a torpedo-guidance system used in World War II, an invention that is now used for Wi-

Fi. Yeah, not only did she master resting bitch face; she was critical in creating the technology that now helps you share your face. Hedy continued to be a man-eating mastermind until her death in 2000 at age eighty-five. In 2014, she was inducted into the National Inventors Hall of Fame.

So the next time somebody calls you "fucking crazy," respond with, "Definitely, but someday you're going to tell people about me."

KNOW WHEN TO GO

Life is all about knowing when to accept reality, throw in the towel, and move on. Grudges, relationships, hard feelings—if something is toxic to your personal growth, acknowledge it, drop it, and get on with it. Don't be that sad, clingy loser who's continually obsessing over what once was or could have been. Don't live your life in "maintenance mode."

What is maintenance mode? Maintenance mode is when somebody falsely maintains the hope of either getting back together or getting even—instead of simply getting over something. People do this all the fucking time. You know why your ex won't give back your stuff? They're in maintenance mode. Rather than accepting the reality that the relationship is fucking done, they're trying to maintain just enough contact with you to hopefully get back with you. Why do individuals do this to themselves? Just give back the fucking crossbow and get on with your fucking life, dude. Don't be like King Ludwig of nineteenth-century Bavaria; he didn't know when to call it quits—and he ended up destroying his life because of it, losing his throne, his castle, and the very individual he was obsessing over.

You see, in 1847, Ludwig met a stage dancer by the name of Lola Montez. She was gorgeous, but also a train wreck of epic proportions, with a long history of dragging dudes along for the tumultuous ride. Despite the clear warning signs, Ludwig gave her a royal home, a royal salary, and even a royal title. Feeling empowered by all that he had bestowed upon her, Lola began to overstep her bounds, abuse her title, and shake shit up in all the wrong ways. She pissed off the nobles, the royal family, and the townsfolk, but Ludwig still kept her around. He couldn't move on; he was too fucking obsessed with her. So in 1848, just a year after the king and Lola met, the lords of Bavaria forced King Ludwig to step down from his royal throne. Then Lola left him. (Because nobody wants to date a has-been.)

In short, don't be a fucking dud—don't hang on too long like King Lud. You're better than that (hopefully).

ON TIME AND HONORABLE

Reliability is probably the greatest thing you can contribute to society. Seriously, if you want to be respected, be reliable. And if you want a reputation that goes down for generations—well, reliability will set that foundation. Because when you're reliable, people know what to expect of you. And how the hell can somebody start spreading the legend of you as a person if you're never around to create that legend in the first place? They can't—so stop canceling plans.

My point: In a world growing ever more consumed with social media and instant gratification, everybody wants to be somebody, everyone wants to be well known, but nobody wants to actually be relied upon. And what's more reliable than the mail? Well, traditionally speaking. Again, like other things, the mail ain't what it used to be. But maybe that's only because the United States Postal Service no longer employs individuals like Mary Fields, a.k.a. Stagecoach Mary.

At the age of sixty-three, Mary tried out to become a contracted postal carrier for a Star Route (a term used for low-population routes assigned to contractors) in rural-ass Montana, departing from the town of Cascade. She got the gig because her proficiency in horse hitching was the quickest of all who auditioned. Now, although her route was far too difficult to allow for a stagecoach to be used, she got the nickname Stagecoach Mary because she was just as reliable as the mail teams with the easier routes that could be completed by stagecoach. In other words, Mary and her trusted mule, Moses, were fucking badasses.

In addition to her reliable reputation, Mary was popular with the Native American tribes of the area (and the townsfolk) for her whiskey-drinking, foulmouthed demeanor. So when Montana passed a law banning women from saloons, Mary was granted an exception by the mayor himself—making her not only the FIRST African American woman to work for the postal service but also the ONLY woman in Montana legally allowed to get publicly wasted. Seriously, people fucking loved Mary; she was asked to babysit, given free meals at local restaurants, and treated like the coolest grandmother anyone could ask for.

Then in 1903, at the age of seventy-one—after eight years of handling the mail for one of Montana's toughest letter-bearing areas—Mary retired from her postal role. She died on December 5, 1914, and her funeral set the town record for the largest attendance ever. (Something tells me the following day was probably the town's most hungover day ever as well.)

You see, reliability is the basis of the best reputations. And it's never too late to stop being a flake and start being fucking great.

SEXUAL SWORDPLAY

S-E-X. You know, knocking boots, tappin' ass, answering the bone phone—whatever you choose to call it, no topic in society is discussed as often as sex. As humans, we're simply obsessed with it. So naturally, sexual innuendos have found their way into pretty much every aspect of life over the years. Albeit, some of these innuendos were made far more obvious than others.

For example, single girls in nineteenth-century Finland would attend parties wearing an empty sword or dagger sheath around their waist. The single men in attendance, well, they'd slip their sword into the sheath of whichever girl they were interested in "getting to know." The girl could then decide to either remove the sword and return it to the potential suitor or let the sword stay and allow the man to take an actual stab at her. Oh, and they were also now engaged. Yeah, engaged. A sword in the sheath was a marriage proposal. How fucking lame of a proposal is that? Imagine going to a bar as a single female nowadays if this same dating ritual were practiced; there is absolutely no fucking way you'd leave without a fiancé.

Your mom would be like, "So, how did you guys meet?" And your answer would be, "Silly story, Mom. I got drunk at a bar and thought I was carrying the sword of this tall, handsome doctor I was talking to earlier in the night. So yeah, I didn't return it, but, like, it wasn't. Anyway, now

Kyle and I are engaged—surprise!" Then your dad would be like, "Goddamnit, Lindsey." And you'd be married to some piece-of-shit wannabe DJ for the rest of your life. Terrible, just terrible.

Now, aren't you glad guys at bars are only trying to poke you with a weird appendage instead of an actual sword? The latter sounds pretty fucking dangerous.

SPREADING BLAME

Chlamydia, herpes, gonorrhea, syphilis—no, these aren't fancy celebrity baby names. They're obviously STDs, and they're far more popular than any celebrity could ever be. But where did they come from? Who was the first dude with crotch crickets? Who's to blame for the spread of genital grease? Well, if you're ready and willing to learn, you've come to the right place. Although I'd advise you to use protection as we move forward.

You see, the medieval times were not only full of land wars; they were full of personal wars. The kind of personal wars fought below the belt and behind closed doors. And dragons did exist—except they weren't the big, menacing, fire-breathing monsters you'd like to imagine. Dragons were actually just scaly dicks caused by syphilis, and the fire-breathing was a burning sensation experienced while trying to piss.

Named after the mythological Greek shepherd Syphilus—a man who was cursed with a horrible disease as punishment for insulting the god Apollo—syphilis first emerged in Europe during the late 1400s. It's believed to have been brought back by Christopher Columbus's crew upon their return from their historic voyage, a.k.a. genocide, of 1492. "Seriously, we all know about the fucked-up shit you did in the Americas, but what in the bloody hell was happening on that boat, Christopher?"

After killing an estimated ten million during the late fifteenth century, syphilis had the doctors of the time so confused and scared that they refused to even write its name. And nobody wanted THEIR country to be blamed for the sour saddle rash. The French called it "Spanish disease," the Spanish called it "Neapolitan disease," the Germans called it "Dutch disease," and so on. (Honestly, I kind of think it was just a way for closed-minded parents to keep their kids from dating foreigners.)

Anyway, it was really just one big blame game (same as today) as STDs continued to spread, evolve, and adhere to all levels of Darwinism—eventually developing into herpes, chlamydia, and extremely clingy boyfriends/girlfriends.

Well, this story definitely won't prevent you from getting one (good luck with that), but at least now you have a better sense of where all the trouser trouble came from. For real, though, thank God for things like condoms and penicillin. Oh, and smart decisions. Make good choices, you dirty, beautiful idiots.

A HEARTFELT AFFAIR

Quality wants quality. Because when you know you're better than the rest, you're simply not going to settle for anything but the best. It's called "having standards," and standards allow you to live up to your potential and find someone on your same level.

Now, I'm not saying close your mind off to every alternative—that's fucking stupid and wrong. What I'm saying is, Don't waste your time with something, or someone, that's clearly not worth it. Food, fashion, or future companions—whatever it is—ALWAYS choose character over convenience. Because just like you don't want to eat something terribly bland, you sure as shit don't want to have your pants split when you stand or be stuck holding some awful human's hand. The good news: If your pants split, at least those squats are paying off. Powerful legs aside, if you're looking to form a power couple (who isn't?), keep your standards on the forefront of your companion hunt. Speaking of power couples, have you met Mary and Percy? Well, you're about to.

The year is 1814 and Mary Godwin, English novelist and daughter of the famous Mary Wollstonecraft, has just met Percy Shelley, one of the most influential English poets of all time. Together these two word nerds traveled throughout Europe, both weird as fucking shit and both with an absolute admiration for each other's work and talent. In 1816, they married. In 1817, Mary completed writing a little 280-page novel titled *Frankenstein*. Actually, the full name at the time was *Frankenstein; or, The Modern Prometheus*. And, well, the book was a fucking hit, launching Mary into unforeseen fame. (If you haven't read it, you should; the monster she created is much cooler than the ones you've dated.)

Sadly, Percy drowned in a boating accident in 1822, after which Mary became a highly sought-after woman. In 1826, even the actor John Howard Payne proposed to her, but Mary roasted him with this response: "I was married to a genius, I could only marry another." She wasn't about to waste her time with anything but the best. Instead, she went on to author another six novels, dozens of short stories, and countless literary articles. She never remarried. Upon her death, Percy's heart was discovered in one of the drawers of her desk, wrapped in pages of some of his final poems. Although Percy's body was cremated, his heart didn't burn. Some people undoubtedly saw this as a sign of never-ending love, but with today's medical knowledge, this would be attributed to calcification due to tuberculosis.

Moral of the story: If you find someone of quality, keep their heart in a drawer. Wait until they die first though—and don't kill them to make this happen. That kind of behavior belongs in one of Mary's books. For you, it's not a good look.

YOUR DOG KNOWS BEST

They say dogs can smell fear, but do you know what else they can smell? Bullshit. If your dog doesn't like somebody, it's because that person is a fucking loser. And if a dog doesn't like you, well, it's probably not the first time you've failed to make new friends. Humans have been using dogs as dickhead detectors for centuries. The Irish definitely did, and as early as the fifth century, they began adding the prefix "Cu" to the names of the noble kings and warriors who had proven themselves worthy of a dog's loyalty and affection. That way, you could immediately recognize the good guys because of their "Cu" title.

Take, for example, Cu Chonnacht O'Reilly, lord of Bréifne Ó Raghallaigh. In simpler terms, he was the king of Bréifne. Basically, this dude was a king who owned some badass dogs. And the "Cu" before his name means he had earned the trust, love, and affection of those badass dogs. Thus, he was a man you could trust. In other words, if you met a noble without the "Cu" before his name, he might be a cat owner and was somebody you should probably run from.

Basically, cat owners are fucking sketchy, and the Irish knew this. You want to be a king? Get a fucking dog. You want people to love, honor, and respect you? Adopt a puppy. You want the world to know you're one of the good guys? Strut with your mutt. But if you want to be a weird, antisocial lowlife—living in a small basement apartment

while eating undercooked TV dinners and plotting the demise of your enemies—get a cat. Stroke it, talk to it, and together you can watch your evil plans fail again and again. Nobody ever defeated their enemies with an animal that rhymes with mittens.

Well, there you have it. You just learned some hound history. So the next time you meet someone who claims they're "not a dog person," report them to the authorities—immediately—because they're probably a terrorist.

PARISIAN PROSTITUTION

To continue our discussion on dogs, like most great things, the French bulldog is the result of selective breeding—kind of like the creation of Hot Pockets. Little bit of this, little bit of that, and eventually you end up with something wonderful. But what you probably don't know about these stubby little bat dogs is they largely gained their popularity in the mid-1800s as the go-to accessory for socialites and streetwalkers to exude class and thus, attract men. And yes, "streetwalker" means prostitute. If you ask me, these ladies were fucking smart. Nobody can resist a French bulldog. Everybody—man, woman, and beast—is going to approach you if you have one of these little dudes on a leash. And that created the perfect opportunity to seal the deal and make a little money. French bulldogs were basically the working girl's wingman.

Given the information I just presented about nineteenth-century French culture, it was safe to assume that if you saw a lady walking down the street with her Hot Pocket creation of a dog, there was a pretty good chance—with a little bit of money and some sweet talking—you could negotiate your way into her "hot pocket." Now, fast-forward to today: I'm not saying every girl who owns a French bulldog is a hooker, but there's a pretty good chance she is. I'd say something like 80/20. The 20 percent being the girls who are just trying to look rough around the edges—it's called streetwalker chic. And you know what? I love it. Because as humans, we all have two basic needs: the need to pet dogs and the need to touch butts. So for that reason, any girl who owns a French bulldog is a girl I'd like to know.

DISCLAIMER: It's totally not my fault if you get punched in the dick for approaching a girl with a French bulldog assuming she's a prostitute. Times have changed (I think).

DON'T LOSE SIGHT OF YOURSELF

Straight up, nobody in this world is worth losing your shit over. There's no reason to act jealous, be possessive, or allow yourself to become sad and desperate. If someone doesn't like you, who fucking cares? Find someone who does. If your significant other makes you feel like shit, they're fucking shit—bury them in a sandbox, forget about 'em, and move on. Don't be like Joanna of Castile. Don't ruin your life and your reputation with an insecure obsession.

Born in 1479, Joanna (Spanish spelling: Juana) was the third child of Queen Isabella of Castile and King Ferdinand II of Aragon. But this royal privilege didn't stop her from working hard to improve herself. As a young woman, she spoke six languages, excelled in religious studies, was active in equestrian sports, played music, and could dance with the best of them. Plain and simple, Joanna was a fucking badass. She was smart AND beautiful; this obviously attracted the attention of men. And in 1496 she married Philip of Habsburg, also known as Philip the Handsome. Seri-

ously, the dude's nickname was PHILIP THE HANDSOME—are you fucking kidding me? He must have looked like Idris Elba and Ryan Gosling had a baby the height of Dwayne "the Rock" Johnson. My point, even Philip's handsome ass wasn't worth "losing it." But Joanna couldn't resist, she let her imagination get the best of her, and she became absolutely paranoid he was going to cheat.

Her insecurities intensified, and her mental instability grew ever more apparent around the kingdom. She was like a fucking vulture, constantly swarming over Philip, checking his iPhone, and demanding his email passwords. Needless to say, it was sad to watch. She was once such a smart, intelligent, confident woman. Not even Philip's surprise death in 1506 quelled her insecurities. She wouldn't allow nuns to approach his corpse before his burial—afraid he'd put his ghost boner in one of them.

In the end, Joanna of Castile became known as Joanna the Mad, leaving behind a reputation of being pathetically jealous instead of beautifully badass.

OUTWIT AND OUTLIVE

Sometimes life is going to kick you in the balls, boobs, or another soft area on the body that isn't built to take a blow. Basically, if it feels good to be touched there during sex, it's going to hurt like hell when life delivers a reality check.

We've all had a day, a week, or even a year when it feels like life is simply out to get us. But whatever you're going through, mental stamina will prevent life from getting the best of you. You're going to have to get creative, you're going to have to take some risks, and you're going to have to do whatever's within your power to get through life's bullshit. Let me illustrate this idea by taking you on a trek back to the fourteenth century.

Here we meet Countess Loretta of Sponheim, the wife of Heinrich II, Count of Sponheim (an independent county in what is now Germany). In 1323, Heinrich died of disease, leaving Loretta with three young sons and a kingdom to run. Adding worry to widowhood, this all happened during a time of widespread poverty, conflict, and economic depression across the land. But miraculously, Loretta managed to keep it together, and she was feeling optimistic about the future.

Then in 1328, Baldwin of Luxembourg—an archbishop and the brother of Holy Roman emperor Henry VII—claimed he owned Loretta's land and wanted it back. Not willing to give in and give away the land she'd worked to maintain, she got creative and took a risk: She had Baldwin's ass kidnapped. She proceeded to hold him hostage until he changed his mind, ceded his land claims, and even helped raise a large ransom to regain his freedom.

Loretta continued to rule Sponheim alone until her eldest son was old enough to take the throne, which was sometime around 1330. She used funds left over from the kidnapping plot to build herself a huge castle, a castle she named Frauenberg—translation: "Lady Castle." ("Lady Castle" definitely sounds like a nickname for one of those tender body parts we were talking about earlier. And honestly, any dude lucky enough to get in there should treat it with the same respect.)

Anyway, Loretta lived in Lady Castle until her death in 1346. The lesson from all this: The next time someone tries to take a cheap shot, think like Loretta, and you'll come out on top.

A RIDE WORTH REMEMBERING

Some days seem to drag on forever, testing the patience of even the most angelic among us. (I've even heard my mother swear during one of these particularly cuss-worthy, never-ending days.) And some nights can seem to last even longer. You ever been at a party that you didn't want to attend? Minutes feel like hours, and those hours feel like, well, torture. But sometimes that's the length you have to go to in order to support a friend or appear social long enough to meet a decent man/woman. And on that note, let's talk a bit about length.

No, we're not going to talk about THAT kind of length. If you're looking to read about "measuring up," get on Facebook and check out another one of your aunt's TMI posts about the type of guy she's looking to meet on a Christian dating site. (What does "Bible-worthy below the belt" even mean?) Rather, we're going to talk about the length one rider was willing to go to warn of an impending British invasion, demon-strating the kind of grit it's going to take for you to survive your next all-nighter.

Now, I'm sure you think I'm about to tell you the story of some guy whose name rhymes with "tall, cold beer," but what that guy did isn't impressive enough for the pages of this book. Instead, I'm going to tell you about a rider who rode nearly twice the motherfucking distance of our beer-buddy Paul. Her name was Sybil Ludington, and in 1777 she was just sixteen years old when she rode 40 miles in the dead of night—armed with only a stick—to alarm the militia of incoming British troops (for comparison, Paul rode 21.7 miles).

I don't know if you've ever ridden a horse before, but 40 continuous miles on horseback is far more difficult than anything you've ever done involving a squat rack.

In doing so, Sybil was personally thanked—by a fairly popular general named George Washington (maybe you've heard of him)—for her role in helping push the British back to their ships during the American Revolutionary War. The bad news: The story of her ride didn't become common knowledge until the early 1900s. The good news: There's now a badass statue of her located in a park in Carmel, New York.

Anyway, if Sybil could ride all night, you can certainly keep your antisocial ass out past midnight.

JAILHOUSE WEDLOCK

Weddings, birthdays, graduations, holidays—these milestone moments bring together family. A chance to gather, eat, and dodge the inevitable "So why aren't you married yet?" question you'll be asked by relatives you forgot even existed. As if you weren't already self-conscious enough about your dating life, now you have people who are complete fucking strangers 364 days of the year questioning your "dateability." Who the fuck does Aunt Karen think she is anyway? She's been divorced four times; she's the last person who should be questioning you. Regardless, she's doing it—so how do you answer? Well, your answer should begin by expressing the fact that you're just waiting for the "right one." You know, one of those timeless, romantic encounters that can happen only in a city like Paris.

The year is 1719, and dozens of "undateable" women are about to meet the man of their dreams, get married, and be sent on an all-expenses-paid honeymoon to America. Because this is the year the French government offered male prisoners release if they agreed to do one simple thing as a condition of their liberation: Marry a prostitute and move to Louisiana. Yeah, even the French knew marriage is a punishment worse than prison. Pretty fucking romantic though, right? I mean, you had all these working girls, who had likely given up on finding a guy, suddenly married to a prison-sculpted hard bod—some real *Pretty Woman* kind of shit. (No wonder Paris is known as the City of Love.)

Now, it wasn't just criminals and call girls being sent to Louisiana (chained together, by the way—a literal "ball and chain" type of marriage); the French government also sent the homeless, and some families even sent their troubled teens.

Essentially, deportation to Louisiana was done in an attempt to clean up the city. All in all, hundreds of Parisians became southern-state castaways during the early 1700s. But hey, at least some ladies got a husband out of it.

So the next time they ask that dreaded question, let your relatives know you're just waiting for a French felon to come sweep you off your feet. Then, with a mouthful of mashed potatoes, share this story with them. There's still hope for you.

A HAIRY PROPOSITION

Everybody enjoys a good hat. The convenience of leaving your home without feeling the need to run a comb through your hair beforehand is just awesome. But back in nineteenth-century Victorian Britain, the men didn't wear hats just to cover their hair—they wore hats to show off their lover's hair. Yeah, you read that right. Doesn't seem to make sense, does it?

Believe it or not, there was actually a time when giving someone a chunk of your crotch wig was considered a sign of affection—a sign of affection that men proudly displayed, pinning their lover's pubic hair to their hat like a trophy. (Perfectly reasonable. If you go to third base, you want to bring back a souvenir.) The best part about this was that you'd never have to wonder whether the carpet matched the drapes; you'd know for sure what everyone had going on—hat hair tells no lies. Plus, for girls, it would be super easy to catch your dude cheating on you. It would happen like this: "Karl! Whose fucking clam hair is this pinned to your hat!? These aren't my curls, you two-timing son of a bitch!" And just like that, your marriage is over. ("Karl, you fucking jerk.")

Anyway, chances are you have trouble even getting your boyfriend to wear that shirt you bought him last Valentine's Day. Now imagine trying to get him to wear a tuft of pubes on his head. THAT would be a true measure of his love. You should probably ask him to do it. And I'm talking real pubes—not that shitty attempt at a beard he already has on his face.

If dudes 150 years ago could wear biscuit whiskers to show their commitment, surely your boyfriend can do it. It's so much more meaningful than a name tattoo. Trust me—I have one of those, and Ashley doesn't mean a thing to me.

STEP YOUR GAME UP

Everybody loves surprises. Think outside the bin with your next romantic gesture. Seriously, what the fuck is your girlfriend going to do with a fifty-two-inch teddy bear anyway? C'mon, use your imagination for something other than dreaming about a rap career for once. Your poor girl has been putting up with your shit for months—maybe even years—and all you can do is get her something from the front bin of your local Walmart? That's just wrong.

Let's set the bar with a historical example of a dude going all in for his girl: The year is 1931, and King Edward VIII (at this time, he was just Prince Edward) meets a married American woman by the name of Wallis Simpson. They hit it off, they frequent the bone zone together for a number of years, and Edward is convinced she is "the one." Wallis, feeling equally as passionate, obtains a divorce and gets ready to put her wifey lock on Edward's crown jewels. At this same time, in early 1936, Edward's dad dies, and Prince Edward becomes King Edward. Now this is where it gets complicated.

Edward and Ms. Simpson's little arrangement is met with heavy opposition by the British government on all kinds of legal, political, religious, and moral grounds. The gist of it: As king of England, Edward was not allowed to marry a divorced woman, because it was against the beliefs of the Church of England. So what did Edward do? He gave up his throne.

Yeah, the dude gave up his position as THE KING OF MOTHERFUCKING ENGLAND just so he could marry Ms. Simpson. And the two lived the remainder of their lives together in the beautiful French countryside.

Now, Edward may have given up his position as king of England, but in terms of romantic gestures, Edward will always be the king. In other words, step your game up, teddy-bear boy.

ROMANTIC REVENGE

Lady lovers, if you're lucky enough to land yourself a badass girl, you better hold on to her. Hold on to her the way you clutch a hundred-dollar bill, a gift card to your favorite restaurant, or anything else you find as important as food and money. Because you know what they say: You don't know what you have until it's gone.

So just how does one go about finding one of these elusive, unwavering creatures of badassness? Online dating? Nope. (Well, unless you want to date your fucking cousin or someone you went to high school with—equally disgusting options.) Your best bet is probably going to be in person. Perhaps through a friend of a friend, but most likely it will happen when you least expect it. You might even die before you have a chance to realize how badass your girl really is. Take, for example, Jeanne de Clisson, also known as the Lioness of Brittany.

If that nickname doesn't prove just how badass this woman was, let me tell you a little more about her: In 1330, Jeanne married Olivier de Clisson IV, a wealthy Breton lord and son of a military legend. And like all political couples, Olivier and Jeanne were under fervent, unrelenting scrutiny. In fact, in 1343, this resulted in Olivier being arrested by his own countrymen regarding a previous conflict he'd had with the English. He was put on trial, found guilty, and beheaded on August 2, 1343. (Yeah, there wasn't much of an appeal process back then.)

Appalled by the unjust treatment and execution of her beloved husband, Jeanne swore to avenge his death. So she purchased three ships, painted them black, dyed the sails blood red, and became a fucking pirate. She then hired a crew along with two sons she shared with Olivier, and together the family pursued and captured French fleets. (Way better than a family road trip.) As each new ship was captured, Jeanne would board the vessel and proceed to personally chop the French nobles' heads off with a fucking ax—a tribute to the way French nobility had killed her husband.

Now, if you're debating whether you should marry your current girlfriend, ask just how far she's willing to go to avenge your death. That's a great test of badassness. And if you have yourself a Jeanne, you better get that girl a ring.

KEEP IT PRIVATE

Couples. Some of them are disgusting: The ones who are always kissing, sitting on the same side of a booth, sharing entrées, finishing each other's sentences, wearing matching outfits, using pet names, and doing a multitude of other obnoxious PG-rated acts of love. Seriously though, if you're going to get down with some public displays of affection, at least make it worth watching for the rest of us. Either make me horny or make your way into a car and go the fuck home, you cute, gross, disgusting lovebirds.

But whatever you do, don't go fighting and arguing in public, because there's nothing more uncomfortable or inappropriate than airing your dirty laundry in front of an audience. And yes, social media does count as "in public." Besides, you're probably arguing about some dumb, boring-couple shit anyway. Speaking of that, I feel it's my duty to inform you that there are no rules when it comes to jumping ahead to the next episode of a series you started together. There's no "together" when it comes to binge-watching, binge-drinking, or binge-eating; it's every man, woman, or gender-neutral individual for themselves.

You know who's great at keeping their arguments quiet? Mimes. You know who else was great at this? Thomas Fucking Edison. (Yeah, the light bulb guy.) You see, after Thomas married his second wife, Mina Miller, in 1886, he taught her Morse code so that they could communicate with finger tapping while holding hands—allowing them to have a private conversation in a crowded room. It was kind of like texting when you're sitting right next to each other, except way cooler because it's fucking Morse code and it requires you to actually be smart and not just own a smartphone. My point: Thomas Edison was a smart guy. And as a smart guy, he knew that not everybody needed to hear his private conversations with his wife. You should do the same thing. Be smart. Be like Thomas and keep party gossip between the two of you.

Now, enjoy the rest of your day, and start practicing your Morse code, which will give the phrase "tap that" an entirely new meaning in your relationship.

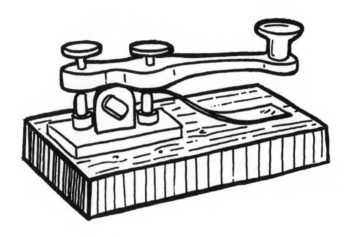

A PROVOKING SMOKE

There's nothing in life worse than feeling controlled. Whether it's your boss telling you to stop dyeing your hair blue or a possessive boyfriend/girlfriend telling you to unfollow somebody you once knew, being told how to act is fucking annoying. And sometimes it's downright fucking wrong. Unfortunately, this isn't always something you can avoid. Some people and organizations will always attempt to control you in some way or another—that part is out of your control. However, what you can control is how you react. If you don't like something, let it be known. Because that is the only way to set the proper tone moving forward. Take, for example, Katie Mulcahey.

On January 22, 1908, Ms. Mulcahey was arrested in New York City's Bowery district for smoking a cigarette in public. Which, at the time, was illegal under the Sullivan Ordinance, a dumb law created by some lame-ass union to ban women—and only women—from public inhalation. Basically, some self-righteous fucks decided that ladies who smoke must be "immoral and loose." In other words, "too much fucking fun for public consumption." So they passed a hypocritical law to preserve the purity of New York's female populace. Katie, in all her impure glory, broke that law. And she had this to say to the judge: "I've got

as much right to smoke as you have. I never heard of this new law, and I don't want to hear about it. No man shall dictate to me."

Well, the judge didn't like the feeling of his balls shriveling up inside him, so Katie was found guilty and fined $5 (roughly $150 today). But Katie didn't give a fuck; she was just getting started. In fact, she stirred up enough shit after the verdict to garner the attention of the mayor. Just two weeks after Katie's arrest, the mayor vetoed the anti-smoking law, and women were once again allowed to get their smoke on. Fuck Columbus Day, where's our Katie Mulcahey Day?

So the next time somebody tries to tell you what to do, think to yourself, "WWKD?" Then use your best outside voice to tell them which direction to fuck (usually the opposite of "on").

CRAZY-LADY BAY

A lot of girls like to joke about being a handful, but the truth is, you probably fucking are. Fortunately, plenty of dudes dig the shit out of girls who are slightly off their rockers. There's something oddly rewarding about being able to handle a girl no one else can. It's like being a pirate, and crazy girls are like an ocean—full of sharks, salt-water crocodiles, jellyfish, and a bunch of other shit that will totally fucking kill you. But if you know how to navigate her deadly, crazy-lady waters, you'll reach an island filled with treasures. Treasures like exciting conversations, R-rated movies, and sex on a Tuesday. Sounds awesome, right? Of course it does.

Granted, dating a lady like this requires a man to always maintain a good sense of humor about life—a life she will gladly end if he's not careful. Take, for example, the great German poet Heinrich Heine. You see, in 1830 (some say 1831), Heinrich left Germany and moved to Paris because the German government wasn't exactly fond of his controversial writing. In fact, shortly after his voluntary departure, the government banned him from ever returning. So what? He was in Paris—way cooler anyway. It was here that he met a young woman named Crescence Eugénie Mirat. Now keep in mind, Heine was a German poet, Crescence didn't speak any German, and she had absolutely no interest in reading or writing. She was pretty much the exact opposite of everything he lived for. So he didn't exactly choose a woman who would be easy to deal with. But they made it work, and they were married in 1841. They stayed together until Heinrich's death in 1856. And in his will, we get a taste of the sense of humor that was necessary to make their relationship work all those years.

In that will, Heinrich left her all his wealth, but with a catch: She had to remarry in order to receive it. Why did he want her to remarry? Because in Heinrich's words, "Then there will be at least one man to regret my death." You see, Heine knew that his wife was a pain in the ass and thought that it would be funny to watch another man try to deal with her shit. Anyway, she quickly remarried. You know, because money is cool and stuff. But I'm sure he floated around as a ghost on all her first dates like, "Oh no he didn't."

Anyway, dudes, don't let anybody—not even a fucking ghost—stop you from sailing into Crazy Lady Bay. It's totally worth it.

GET IT, GIRL

Like coming between a bear and her cubs, coming between a girl and her goals is a recipe for fucking disaster. If a woman's mind is set on something, whether it's the pursuit of a career goal or much-needed carbohydrates, it's fucking on. And in recent times, I can't think of a goal-driven woman who brought it harder than Emmeline Pankhurst, a revolutionary leader of the British women's suffrage movement.

Following the death of her husband in 1898, Emmeline was left a single mother of five. Her husband had always been her strongest supporter, but now, without him, she was forced to pursue her dream of equal voting rights for British women on her own. So in 1903 she formed the Women's Social and Political Union.

Now, one important thing to note about Emmeline: She wasn't about clever rhymes and picket signs. She was a woman of action who lived by the motto "Deeds, not words." What kind of deeds exactly? Well, in 1912, Emmeline was arrested twelve times for arson, vandalism, and other hoodrat things she did to bring attention to her fight. TWELVE FUCKING TIMES—in ONE year. Your favorite rappers don't have shit on Emmeline's level of street cred. With her background, she could have easily dropped a mixtape if she so chose. Something like *Guilty of Being a G* would have been an appropriate title.

I mean, talk about a woman who literally did not give a fuck. Not even one. In a court appearance following one of her arrests, she said, "We are here not because we are lawbreakers; we are here in our efforts to become lawmakers." You see what I'm saying about never getting in the way of a determined woman and her goals? No matter what, she never lost sight of her goal. All she wanted was equal voting rights, and she fought for that goal until the day she died: June 14, 1928, at the age of sixty-nine. (Ha, classic. Sixty-nine—even her death age was rebellious.) And just weeks after her death, the Equal Franchise Act was passed, allowing all British women over twenty-one to vote, regardless of property and marital status.

So the next time you and your friends can't decide on where to eat, TAKE A VOTE. If you're not happy with the outcome, do what Emmeline would do and set something on fire.

FIGHTING FOR THE RIGHT

"Free the nipple." You've seen the hashtag, you've read the posts. And you know what? I'm totally on board with it. Why? Duh, because nipples are fucking cool; they're second only to side boob. (Side boob wins every time.) The way I see it, if you're happy with the size, shape, and spacing of your milk duds, you should definitely be allowed to share them when and wherever you want (if that's your thing). It's a personal choice. Unfortunately, it's a choice reserved only for men. Which is wrong, because dude nipples are fucking dumb and ugly. You can't even milk a dude. (Yeah, your boyfriend really is fucking worthless.) However, there was a time when even men weren't allowed to expose their gumdrops in public.

The Civil War wasn't the only war fought on North American soil. The Nipple Wars of the 1930s were equally as brutal, but involved far less bloodshed. Let's hear about one of these terrifying battles and the brave men who fought for your right to party with your shirt off. The year was 1936, and it was a particularly hot day up in America's toupee, a.k.a. Toronto, Canada. So hot that many men decided to bare their chests at a local beach (fucking rebels). This rogue move resulted in thirty men being arrested for indecent exposure. I mean, I've heard of some pretty weird shit coming out of Canada—like polite criminals and affordable health care—but this story really takes the Canadian cake. FYI: A "Canadian cake" is a slang term I just made up for a birthday party that involves beer, fistfights, and pouring brown gravy on FUCKING EVERYTHING. (Canadians will get it.) Now, in Canada's defense, men were fighting the same fight in New York City at that time as well. Basically, in 1936 we were all prudes.

Anyway, shortly after the Toronto Titty Gang members were arrested, the laws were changed, and it was finally deemed acceptable for men to go topless. Thus, the first major victory of the North American Nipple Wars was won.

Fast-forward to today. What's so offensive about female nipples anyway? I say, free the female nipple, hide the fucking bro toes. If you want to talk about something offensive, let's talk about dudes wearing sandals. Fuck flip-flops.

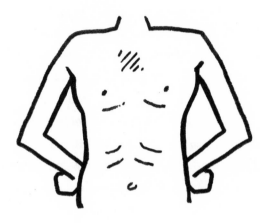

LAWS, LIARS, AND LIBATIONS

Some dudes will say just about anything to get laid. They're absolutely relentless with unoriginal compliments, career lies, and anything else they think will help them get horizontal. Any woman who's left her house long enough to go to a bar, club, or pet store knows what I'm talking about. Shit like, "I don't usually talk to girls at bars," "I'm not like other guys," and "I read books." Lies, lies, lies—he just wants a piece of your apple pie. (We already learned about "apple allure" earlier in this book.)

Anyway, the tactic of lying for lady bits—also referred to as "spitting game"—is as old as time. Your dad did it to your mom, and Adam probably did it to Eve. (I don't think her leaf just fell off.) At one point, laws were even passed in an attempt to prevent this behavior by making it illegal for men to bullshit their way into bed. Known as Anti-Seduction Acts, or Seduction Laws, these ordinances were passed in states such as New York, Virginia, Ohio, and Georgia during the 1800s. Each state had its own take on seduction policy, but the one thing they all had in common: Seduction laws applied to the false promise of marriage. Ha, really? How fucking desperate is that? One minute he's buying you a drink and lying about his career as an astronaut, and the next he's throwing out the mother of all Hail Marys and asking for your hand in marriage.

Now, the really stupid thing about these laws is that they assumed women couldn't already sniff out some bullshit. Like somehow a false marriage proposal was a hypnotic guarantee of gettin' some. I don't know about you, but I'm pretty sure girls don't need legal legislation to help them avoid a douche. I mean, I've spent a fair amount of time in Las Vegas, and from what I've seen, women are perfectly capable of navigating douchey waters.

Girls, if a guy simply won't stop trying to get into your honeypot, you're in luck, because there's still a law for you: Newton's law of universal gravitation. This law states that if you hold your drink above a man's head and rotate it sideways, the contents within will do the work of getting rid of him.

A MUTUAL UNDERSTANDING

"So, what are we?" The dreaded question nobody wants to hear from someone they think they're just casually dating. "Are you my friend, my fish friend, my girlfriend, or my half-fish friend who happens to also be a girl?" Yeah, dating a mermaid would be fucking confusing.

Now, I don't care whether you're a man, woman, or mythical sea harlot—discussing your expectations within a relationship is necessary. If you don't want something serious, just be honest about it. Don't let the other person think it's something it's not, as they run around telling everyone the two of you are "dating" when really all you did was split an appetizer a few weeks back. One-sided relationships are bullshit and sad—like the very one-sided relationship between King George III of Great Britain and Elizabeth Spencer.

You see, King George was obsessed with Elizabeth. So obsessed that one day he decided he was no longer married to his actual wife, Queen Charlotte, and instead started telling everyone that he was married to Elizabeth and that Charlotte was a spy trying to kill him. Obviously, embarrassing the hell out of both women. The entire time, Elizabeth was probably like, "George, why are you so obsessed with me?" She literally wanted nothing to do with him, but that didn't stop George from telling everyone about their new relationship. It's worth mentioning that at this time George had also begun to suffer from a rare blood disease known as porphyria, causing him to experience bouts of severe dementia. (Makes sense. Because you literally have to be fucking insane to want to get married—twice.)

Anyway, long story short: Porphyria eventually got the best of ole Georgie boy several years later, and he died on January 29, 1820, Leaving behind one real widow and, well, one fictitious one.

Clearly, not coming to a mutual understanding about what you are as a couple is just embarrassing and awkward for everyone involved.

P-P-P-P-POWER

Vaginas are powerful. Let's be honest, women are basically walking around with an atomic bomb between their legs. And with that kind of power comes the ability to command absolute fear, respect, and devotion. Like Queen Njinga (a.k.a. Nzinga) of Angola did during her reign in the 1600s. Her story begins during the height of the Portuguese slave trade.

Shortly after the death of her father, King Kiluanji, in 1618, her brother took to the throne, but his lack of leadership skills quickly became apparent. So he simply gave up. He killed himself in 1626, allowing the Portuguese to essentially do whatever the fuck they wanted with the Angolan population. And, well, Njinga wasn't about that life. She took control, assumed the throne, and began her retaliation against the Portuguese oppression. Her ruthlessly independent nature made her a brilliant military leader as she organized guerrilla armies to defend her people. Her independent spirit also meant that instead of finding a man to become the new king, she simply took on the role herself, requiring that she be referred to as "King" not "Queen."

And like most kings did back then, she amassed herself a large harem: hundreds of male concubines kept around solely for her sexual pleasure. Now, you wouldn't expect a woman of her status to let just any dude wet his willy with her, would you? Of course not. So in order to find the right guy for the night, she'd choose two and watch them fight to the death. The winner earned the honor of her royal attention. Then, to prevent him from getting too clingy, she'd have him killed the following morning. (Damn, not even breakfast or coffee. Harsh.) The pattern continued for nearly forty years: fighting the Portuguese by day, watching dudes fight to have sex with her by night. Her life was like one of those sexy, violent Rihanna music videos.

Now remember, your vagina is kind of a big deal. I'm not saying you should make guys fight to the death for it, but you should definitely make them work a little. I don't know, maybe something involving karate or, better yet, a fucking career.

PET PARENTING 101

Sure, you can call yourself a "dog mom" or a "cat daddy." But the truth is, you're not a fucking parent—you're a kidnapper, and pets are the ultimate example of Stockholm syndrome. I mean, when has your dog ever complained about where you live? Not once. You just randomly brought him home one day like, "Hey, welcome to your new home," and never has he said shit about your dirty laundry, wine-stained carpet, or poorly assembled IKEA furniture set. He simply accepted his new life with a good attitude and a happy tail. So the way I see it, there's no such thing as taking it too far when it comes to being a good parent to your pets. I say, buy them cute clothes, throw them birthday parties, and treat them like a member of the fucking family. That's the least you can do after kidnapping them from their real mom. Just don't do what Mary Toft did—she was fucking crazy.

In 1726, the seemingly normal resident of Surrey, England, took the pet-parenting thing a little too far. You see, Mary Toft had such a weird-ass obsession with rabbits that she would actually stuff bunnies up her vagina and pretend to give birth to them—literally trying to be their mom. (And you that thought visiting your gynecologist was uncomfortable.) She even performed this feat in front of doctors, convincing them she was a legit bunny-birther. In fact, medical professionals began to attribute her miraculous conceptions to "maternal impression," the belief that dreams and obsession could lead to physical changes within a mother's womb.

Mary became an overnight celebrity and even caught the attention of the British royal family. She carried on her hare hoax for months, "giving birth" to at least fifteen bunnies during this time. It wasn't until a politician put her claims under intense investigation that she finally confessed to what she was doing. (Oh, I forgot to tell you, Mary was married. Her husband was the one buying all the bunnies for her to "birth.")

Huh, suddenly becoming a crazy cat lady doesn't seem so crazy, does it? Now if you'll excuse me, I have a dog's birthday party to attend.

BUCKET BRAWLERS

Admit it. If you're in a relationship, you fight about stupid shit. And anything is fair game when it comes to arguing with your significant other: T-shirts, TV shows, toothbrushes—all valid fodder on a Thursday night. Couples are like angry magicians, but instead of pulling rabbits and doves out of thin air, they pull out topics to argue about. Why? Because humans have exceptional imaginations when they're in a relationship. This is why single people hate couples so much. It's not because we're jealous of your love; it's because we know that deep down inside we all possess the potential to become just like you—and we're fucking scared to death about it.

Now, if you're coupled up, you've probably already begun thinking about all the pointless stuff you've argued about this past week. Well, I'm about to one-up you when it comes to pointless combat. The year is 1325, and a war has just erupted between Modena and Bologna, two rival city-states in northern Italy. Why are they fighting? Because of a bucket. Yes, a fucking bucket. You see, a group of drunk soldiers from Modena snuck into Bologna one night and stole the water bucket from the town well. And, well, the Bolognese people weren't about living a no-bucket life, so the war was fucking on.

All in all, the Battle of Zappolino—also known as the War of the Bucket—saw the bloodshed of about four thousand men. Making it actually one of the largest battles of the medieval era. And you thought your silly fights got serious . . . pfft. Did anybody die? Nope. So relax—your fights are basic.

However, much like the asinine arguments you have with your boyfriend or girlfriend, the bucket-stealing incident was simply the final straw and culmination of years of hostility and annoyance. So the next time your boyfriend or girlfriend picks a stupid fight with you, try to understand that it's most likely the apex of their annoyance about something else you've been doing for some time. Like always making them sleep in the wet spot after your sloppy, post-argument, makeup sex. That's such a jerk move. You should definitely be taking turns snoozing in the postcoital puddle—or at least rock-paper-scissors for it . . . best out of three.

PROACTIVE POLITICS

Don't just sit back and let life happen. If you see something you can fix, fix it. If somebody's not pulling their weight, take over. And if you ever find yourself in a boring, dead-end marriage (ew), end it. Or in the case of Princess Sophie Friederike Auguste von Anhalt-Zerbst-Dornburg—yes, that was her actual name—do all three at the same time. What's Sophie's story? Well, I'm obviously about to tell you.

In 1729, Sophie was born of royal blood to the German family of Anhalt, which had powerful Prussian connections. Connections the family used to arrange Sophie's marriage to Peter III, the dude in line to become the next emperor of Russia. However, regardless of his future potential, Sophie wanted nothing to do with Peter. So, she spent much of her time reading history, studying foreign languages, and writing memoirs. In fact, her early writings indicated her complete disdain for Peter and everything he did. Not only was he a pale, ugly, good-for-nothing, drunk idiot (her words, not mine), he was also a terrible fucking leader. His political policies were shit, and he was far from respected. So in 1762, when he finally got possession of the throne as the new Russian emperor (seventeen years into their marriage), Sophie took it upon herself to change her circumstances.

During one of Peter's not-so-secret rendezvous with a lady friend, Sophie was able to convince a group of Russian soldiers to support her instead of her husband. With this army, she had Peter captured at his mistress's home and held hostage until he agreed to abdicate the throne and make Sophie the sole ruler and empress of Russia. He did (and was killed shortly after). Sophie went on to become Russia's MOST POWERFUL and longest-ruling female leader of all fucking time. She ruled from 1762 to 1796 and led Russia into an era of unheard-of prosperity. (Pretty cool, right?)

Oh, did I mention that during all this she changed her name to Catherine? Yes, Sophie became Catherine the Great—perhaps you've heard of her. Remember her story the next time you find yourself stuck in a rut or surrounded by idiots.

FEMALE FEROCITY

Take no shit. Whether it's work, a relationship, or simply your everyday life, if some-body doesn't treat you right, do something about it. Now, if you're female, you'll prob-ably be called a bitch every time you defend yourself. But guess what? It's better to be a bitch than a victim. So stick up for yourself and be like Hannah Duston.

Born in 1657, Hannah grew up in Massachusetts, where she lived a rather un-eventful life until the year 1697. That year, the mother of nine was kidnapped by Abenaki warriors during King William's War. But this wasn't just your typical "Hey, check out my van" kind of kidnapping. Because not only did they burn Hannah's house down so that her family had nowhere to hide; they also killed her newborn child right in front of her. All in all, around twenty-seven colonists were axed, and thirteen more taken captive during the one-night free-for-all. Granted, we know the early colonists did some pretty fucked-up shit and this was likely retaliation, but what Hannah did next is damn impressive.

You see, Hannah wasn't about to just sit back and let them get away with all this. Hannah, like most moms, was a fighter. So that's what she did: fought. After days of being forced to march through the snow, she seized an opportunity to shake shit up as her captors were sleeping. What exactly did she do? Well, she escaped her restraints, got hold of an ax, and FLIPPED THE FUCK OUT—single-handedly killing ten warriors and sending the others running for the hills. (You know, like your last boyfriend ran from the truth and responsibilities.)

If Hannah's not the definition of a "bad bitch," I honestly don't know who is. After her rampage, she helped the other captives escape and led them to a farmhouse, where they were able to take shelter until they had the strength to make the thirty-mile trek back home. (Talk about a crappy camping trip.)

So the next time somebody wrongs you, don't be afraid to harness your inner Mrs. Duston and go absolutely apeshit. Also, this story proves something that I was once told by a good friend: "Postpartum hormones are nothing to fuck with."

NACHO DADDY

Maybe your current girlfriend gave you the kick in the ass you needed to pursue a new job, maybe she provided you with the tough love you needed to stop being such a piece of shit, or maybe she's just really good at building up your manhood and making you believe your dick is bigger than it is—ultimately leading to a better sex life. My point: A lot of good things in life wouldn't happen without men receiving the proper motivation (or inspiration) from their girlfriends, wives, and other women in their lives. And here's fucking proof.

The year was 1943, and a young maître d' named Ignacio Anaya had no idea he was about to change history when a group of hungry, demanding Texan military wives from Fort Duncan entered his restaurant in Piedras Negras, Mexico. What exactly happened? Well, on that particular day at the Victory Club, the chef was nowhere to be found. So Ignacio, immediately recognizing how fucking dangerous a group of hungry women could be, knew that only he could prevent impending disaster. Not being one to shy away from a challenge, he stepped up to the plate.

He went into the back kitchen, found some tortilla chips, grabbed some cheese, sliced some jalapeños, stacked everything together, threw it in an oven, and—just like that—he became the father of nachos. Yep, it was that easy. Why the name "nachos"? Equally as easy: "Nacho" was Ignacio's nickname. (But after all this, I like to think women began calling him "Nacho Daddy." Something like, "Yeah . . . yeah . . . put your cheese right there, Nacho Daddy.")

I, for one, could not be more grateful for what these women inspired Ignacio to accomplish on that day, because I've never seen a nacho plate I didn't want to impregnate. Anyway, word of his creation eventually snuck across the border to Texas, where it quickly became a baseball-stadium staple (you see, immigration is a good thing). Now, who knows? Had it not been for those hungry women, mankind may have never invented nachos. We'd all be eating celery like a bunch of fucking idiots.

So, ladies, the next time you're hungry and giving your boyfriend attitude, let him know you're just trying to motivate him to actually do something with his fucking life—like Ignacio did when he fathered nachos.

THE PIRATE QUEEN

Traveling, drinking, fighting, and prostitution—just another day in the life of the infamous Chinese pirate Captain Cheng I. (Let's not get into the differences of Cantonese and other Chinese dialects; I'm dramatically simplifying these names down for you.)

You see, Cheng commanded one of the largest documented pirate fleets in history, ransacking much of the South China Sea he called home. But even Cheng wanted more from life, so in 1801 he married a prostitute who went by the name Cheng I Sao. Basically, "wife of Cheng." She was not only fucking gorgeous, but she was also equally as good at handling a sword as she was at handling a dick. Oh, and she was EXTREMELY business savvy. Together, the husband-and-wife team pillaged and plundered for six years, expanding their joint empire until 1807, the year Captain Cheng died.

Was this the end of their pirate dynasty? Nope, it was only the beginning. Cheng I Sao assumed the leadership role and picked up right where her husband had left off. Only now, she was going by the name Ching Shih because she was no longer somebody's wife.

Ching Shih continued to build her empire with brute force and sharp wit. She also played dudes like the dumbasses they are when around an attractive woman. (You know, like smart bartenders and servers do.) And within a few years, Ching Shih became the most powerful pirate in history—controlling more than 1,500 ships and a crew of eighty thousand men.

She was like Beyoncé, but with street cred and more boats. In fact, she was so smart and so powerful that the Chinese government eventually gave up trying to defeat her. In 1810, the government offered her complete amnesty if she would simply retire. So she did. As part of the deal, she was allowed to keep all her money, all her fame, and all her power. (Remember what I said earlier about her savvy business sense?)

After retiring, Madame Ching opened a gambling house and just chilled until 1844, dying at the age of sixty-nine as a grandmother and certified badass.

Anyway, remember this story the next time a guy tells you, "It's a man's world."

TANK IT TO 'EM

Bad news doesn't have to be the end of you. Instead, let whatever you're feeling fuel you. Believe me, with some grit and creativity, you can turn any amount of pain, anger, and confusion into a positive and powerful situation. The best way to do this: Get up every day and fucking crush it. I mean, when you're dealt some serious bullshit, what better way to deal with it than to roll right over the top of it? That's what Mariya Oktyabrskaya did.

Born in 1905, Mariya was one of ten children, and she worked most of her life in factories, canneries, etc. In 1925, she married a Soviet officer, and this sparked her interest in mechanics and military machinery. In 1941, her husband was deployed to fight the Nazis in the Battle of Kiev, where he was later killed. Sadly, it took two years for her to learn that Nazi scum had killed her husband—but when she finally did, instead of mourning she got moving. She sold all her possessions and wrote to the Soviet army offering to buy a tank with the money if, and only if, they allowed her to use it. Officials agreed, and she bought herself a T-34 (the Range Rover Sport of the war).

She named the tank Боевая подруга—which translates to "fighting girlfriend"— and after completing five months of training, she started fighting, rolling into her inaugural battle on October 21, 1943. Many of her military peers viewed her presence as nothing more than planned publicity; however, the fighting metal girlfriend was just as fucking deadly and efficient as the human kind of girlfriend, and Mariya was immediately promoted to sergeant (even though she had a bad habit of repairing her tank while under gunfire).

Weeks later, she proved again why she was a better tank operator than most men were, and her streak of tank-driving terror continued until January 17, 1944. This was the day that her tank track was hit with an explosive and she was subsequently shot while fixing it. She died two months later and in death was honored with the Hero of the Soviet Union medal.

Now, stop reading (even though you're about halfway through the book), get going, and go crush your day—start making your place in motherfucking history (the rest of this book will be waiting for you when you're done).

LOOKIN' GOOD, HONEY

Sometimes you don't want to be the one who gets all the attention. Because not all attention is good attention. The pharaohs of ancient Egypt knew this, and you should too. You see, in order to direct undesired attention toward someone other than the royal majesty, pharaohs required servants to smear their own bodies in honey. And I'm not talking about a quick dab of honey behind the ear. Servants were practically forced to bathe in sticky-icky—like a latex bodysuit of bee puke. So what was the reasoning for the head-to-toe sugary rubdown? Well, it was so that flies and other bugs would land on the servants and not the pharaoh. Thus ensuring that the pharaoh always looked fly—instead of being covered in flies. Servants were made into literal flytraps.

Now, going back to what I said earlier about not all attention being good attention, this is perfectly exemplified in groups of friends at bars and clubs around the world. Think about it: When you're out with your girlfriends, sometimes you just want to be left alone to have a good time. You don't want the attention of hovering, drunk barflies (also known as "horny dudes"). But, like the pharaohs, cunning women have found a way to divert the bar bugs away from themselves and onto somebody else—usually one of their friends.

Allow me to illustrate an example using our friend Megan. For this story, we'll say that Megan is the pharaoh of her girl squad. And like a pharaoh, she's rather full of herself. But instead of glazing her friends in honey like a Christmas ham, Megan tells her friends certain outfits look really "cute," even though it's obvious Jenna and Stephanie are going to attract A LOT of undesired attention. So while her friends are getting swarmed by polo shirts with ill-fated pickup lines, Megan is free to relax in the corner—looking like fucking royalty among a sea of friends with bad fashion sense and horrible taste in men. Well played, Megan . . . kind of fucked up, but still well played.

Cool, now you have a sweet Egyptian honey fact to share on your next coffee date so that you can appear more interesting. (Even though you're likely fresh off a nine-day Netflix bender and have completely forgotten how to participate in society.)

THE DEVIL FROM OHIO

If someone calls you "intimidating," it's a compliment. It means you're strong, suc-cessful, outspoken, attractive, or, well, maybe you're just tall—all positive attributes (if you ask me). But for some reason—especially when it comes to dating—being told you're intimidating is often regarded as a bad thing. Why? People call you intimidat-ing only to deflect from their own lack of independence. Don't change for them.

Take, for example, Victoria Woodhull, a.k.a. "Mrs. Satan"—a label bestowed upon her in 1872 by one of her many critics. Now, she didn't get that name because she said dumb stuff like "Coffee as black as my soul." (Life in the 1800s wasn't that kind of basic.) She EARNED that moniker by chopping away at the framework of society and all those who built it. In 1870, Victoria and her sister were the first women to trade on Wall Street (they also started their own newspaper). In 1871, Victoria was the first woman to officially address Congress, speaking on behalf of the women's suffrage movement. AND in 1872, she became the first woman to run for president; however, she was met with heavy opposition from day one and actually spent Elec-tion Day in jail. She was arrested just a few days prior to the big ballot day for articles she'd published in her paper. Hmm . . . rather "timely," don't you think?

But as much as people tried to stop her, Victoria just kept living her life—her way. Even other women's rights leaders, including Susan B. Anthony, described her as "lewd and indecent"—likely due to the fact that Victoria was unabashedly unguarded when it came to talking about her sex life. She lived with her husband, ex-husband, AND "flavor of the month" at the same damn time under the same fucking roof. (Ha. What's that Jay-Z line? "Ladies is pimps too, go and brush your shoulders off"?)

Needless to say, Victoria was also the first woman to truly fight to keep the government focused on politics and not on a woman's privates. Anyway, Mrs. Woodhull was clearly the very definition of "intimidating," and because of that, you're reading about her today. All hail, Mrs. Satan. (Damn that "Mrs." title—the good ones are always taken.)

In closing, let this be a lesson: If anyone calls you a "she-devil," it's an accolade. And you fucking earned it.

SILENCE IS SO SKETCHY

When it comes to fighting with your boyfriend, girlfriend, husband, wife—or whatever the hell you call yourselves in today's confusing culture—know this: Silence is not golden. Actually, silence is a sign of imminent doom. Believe me, it's not so much the silent treatment as much as it's a silent warning. Because when your significant other opts to get quiet, they're doing so in order to plot shit.

The gears in their brain are moving faster than your mouth ever could in an attempt to defend yourself. And that's not even the scariest part about all this; the scariest part is the fact that nobody has any fucking clue what's going to happen the moment that silence breaks—not even them. But whatever it is, know this: It will likely be calculated, clever, and fucking devastating. And nobody learned this lesson or deserved the post-silence repercussions more than the Nazis attempting to defeat the Soviet Air Force's 588th Night Bomber Regiment.

During the height of World War II, this all-female air brigade was perhaps the most feared fleet in the sky. Known to the Nazis as the "Night Witches," this crew of high-flying hell-raisers carried out an estimated thirty thousand missions over the course of four years (meaning each pilot successfully completed about eight hundred air attacks), raining death on their enemies to the tune of twenty-three thousand tons of bombs dropped from planes decorated with hand-painted flowers. They attacked under cover of darkness and with absolute silence. (Sound familiar?) As the ladies approached their Nazi targets, they'd turn off their engines and glide into position with only the sound of the wind over their wings revealing their arrival. And by the time that sound became audible, it was already too fucking late. "Boom,

bang, blam—game over, Nazi man." The Nazis became so afraid
of these nightly raids that they began spreading rumors that
the Russians had developed medicine allowing these
women to see at night, making them true preda-
tors of flight.

Anyway, guys and gals, the next time
your [insert appropriate title here] is giving
you the silent treatment, go to a safe space
and prepare for the worst—bring a snack, because you might be there a while.

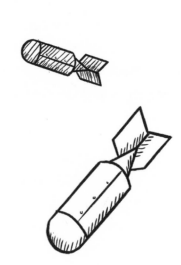

BITING BACK

When we choose and set boundaries—emotional, physical, spiritual, or whatever—we set restrictions on how others can treat us (including ourselves). And what happens when somebody crosses our boundary? Well, we get upset, we get uncomfortable, or perhaps we become utterly fucking "unreasonable." Regardless, setting boundaries is perfectly healthy. In fact, setting boundaries is absolutely fucking necessary. And what better time to set boundaries—and defend those boundaries—than around the holidays?

To illustrate this, here's a story about what happened when somebody crossed a boundary at a holiday party: In 1837, a man by the name of Thomas Saverland was talking to Miss Caroline Newton and her sister at an English pub the day after Christmas. As the three conversed, Caroline's sister shared the news that she had a boyfriend (not in town) to whom she'd made the promise to "not be kissed" while they were apart during the holiday season. And, well, Thomas took this as a challenge and laid one on her. He laughed, Caroline's sister laughed (albeit a bit awkwardly), and Caroline did the exact fucking opposite—she spoke up.

Arrogantly, Thomas felt he was being faced with yet another challenge and said, "If you're angry, I'll kiss you also." But when he attempted to do so, Caroline fought back, and the two fell to the ground. When they regained their footing, Caroline went on the attack. Thomas tried AGAIN to give her a kiss, and Caroline bit off his left nostril. Yep, since he refused to listen after she'd already given him a piece of her mind, she bit off a piece of his fucking nose.

Okay, so you might be wondering why the details of the encounter are so comprehensive. I mean, how the hell could we possibly know what happened at a bar nearly two hundred years ago? (Chances are, you can barely even remember last weekend.) Well, it's because Thomas took Caroline to court after losing part of his nose to her mouthy retort. The incident was recorded by a reporter, and the proceedings became known as the *Saverland v. Newton* case. You'll be happy to hear that the jury found Caroline not guilty, and she was acquitted of all charges after the chairman stated, "Gentlemen, my opinion is, that if a man attempts to kiss a woman against her will, she has a right to bite his nose off, if she has a fancy for doing." In other words, "Suck it, Saverland. You deserve that nostril loss."

Now, I'm not saying you have to start biting people (unless they deserve it), but setting boundaries—and protecting/enforcing those boundaries—is going to come in handy in your life. Especially when somebody starts to get too handsy or, you know, too nosy.

LOAF LOVE AS SELF-LOVE

Breadsticks, pasta bowls, and piles of fries stacked so high that it requires the effort of an entire squad to reach completion—no matter your preference, carbs are fucking delicious. And with the exception of trendy, gluten-fearing freaks, EVERYBODY enjoys the warm embrace of a tortilla or the emotional security that can only be found deep within lasagna's lustful layers; however, as is often the case, too much of a good thing can definitely be bad.

If you drink too much, you'll puke. If you sleep too much, you can say goodbye to your social life. And if you eat too many carbs, you'll experience bloating, remorse, and complete energetic collapse—also known as a "carb coma." Or for all you medical nerds, "postprandial somnolence." Yeah, carb comas are so common that there's a legit medical term for them. (Use that shit the next time you want to impress your friends at brunch. "You guys, I had way too many fries. I can already feel myself slipping into, like, postprandial somnolence.") So by now you're probably wondering, "Why all this carb conversation, Captain?" Well, it's because I want to share with you an interesting sexual act to discuss with your carb-loving compadres at your next gluten-fueled get-together.

If you thought it was impossible for anybody to love carbs more than yourself, you're fucking wrong. Bread-fucking wrong. (Get it? Like, "dead-fucking wrong" but with baking flour instead of funeral flowers.) You see, as far back as the fifth century, the Greeks and the Romans were fucking carbs—yes, literally fucking them—using something known as an olisbokollix. Translation: "bread dildo." Created by intentionally overbaking phallic-shaped breadsticks, they had an entirely different way of expressing their love for carbohydrates. I know it sounds weird, but can you blame these women? They were married to a bunch of dudes wearing togas and sandals—NOBODY wants to have sex with that. Also, there's no such thing as a breadstick drinking too much and getting Greco-Roman wine dick. (Overbaked carbs are always hard and ready to party.)

The next time you hear somebody say, "Oh my God, I love carbs," you now have the information you need to immediately turn it into a discussion about dildos.

PUSSY PLUNDER

Being a pirate takes balls. So naturally you'd assume someone with actual balls would be best at carrying on a pirate legacy, right? Wrong. Take, for example, Grace O'Malley. She didn't just carry on her father's legacy. She took it to new heights and became one of the most dominant women of the sixteenth century, earning the moniker "the Pirate Queen of Connacht." Here's how it happened . . .

Her father, Owen "Black Oak" O'Malley, commanded a fleet of ships that ransomed many of the Irish ports and surrounding trade routes. In other words, they engaged in a lot of piratey activities like stealing and fighting. As a teenager, Grace was anxious to learn the family business and be treated like one of the men. So she chopped off her hair and joined her father's crew. (Not sure what a pixie cut proves, but good for her.) Turns out, she had a knack for seafaring warfare: She was quick-tempered and vindictive, and most importantly, she was fucking smart. She gained the respect of her father's crew and other pirates who heard of her reputation through late-night, rum-induced conversation.

In 1546, Grace married Donal O'Flaherty, the leader of another gang of marauders. Several years and a few children later, Donal was killed, leaving Grace widowed but in command of his entire fleet. This was a natural role for her to assume, since she'd been handling much of his business anyway. Shortly after, she inherited yet another fleet following the death of her father. Meaning, pretty much all of western Ireland's waters were under her ruthless command, and this is when her high-seas reign really began.

Grace held nothing back. If other ships didn't agree to pay her, Grace would raid the vessel and take what she wanted. At one point, Turkish pirates attempted to board her ship while she slept, but Grace got up, shot their captain, boarded his ship, and killed his entire crew. (Let that be a lesson: If you choose to disturb a woman while she naps, there's no telling how much bloodshed it may cause.) Anyway, Grace continued to pillage and plunder for decades—and even got herself a castle—until the English navy could no longer ignore her power and made an attempt to stop her (obviously, unsuccessfully). Grace's relentlessness impressed Queen Elizabeth, and in 1593 the two independent women had a face-to-face meeting. At this rendezvous, Grace received permission to carry on pirating without further English interruption, thanks to mutual understanding and female-to-female admiration. So Grace continued marauding for a few more years. But all good things must come to an end, and Grace retired to Rockfleet Castle, where she died in 1603.

Whether male or female, pirates prove that the course of your life is up to you.

DENIAL ON THE NILE

If you're in it for the credit, you probably shouldn't be in it at all. Because whatever you do, there's no guarantee that your accomplishments will be remembered or recognized anyway. Not to mention, if you do accomplish something great, you're going to stir up a lot of jealousy, envy, and hate. And these feelings can lead people to do some pretty ridiculous shit, like attempting to make others forget about you entirely. This is what happened to Hatshepsut. You ever heard of her? Exactly.

Born fourteen centuries before Cleopatra, Hatshepsut was the daughter of Pharaoh Thutmose I and Queen Ahmose. Around 1492 BC, after the death of her father, Hatshepsut married her half-brother Thutmose II (ew, yucky family fucking), and he became the new pharaoh and Hatshepsut the new queen. However, in 1479 BC, Thutmose II died, and Hatshepsut was appointed queen regent—a.k.a. a seat filler—until her stepson, Thutmose III, could continue the male lineage. But Hatshepsut had royal blood and believed that made her the rightful heir.

In a controversial move, she appointed herself pharaoh in 1478 BC (the exact date is a topic of scholarly debate) and successfully began a twenty-year supremacy that was one of the most prosperous in Egyptian history. She was an aggressive, ambitious, and amicable leader; she didn't rely on bloodshed to get shit done, and she was always focused on what was best for her kingdom. Statues, paintings, and idols were created to honor her—which she often required be made with huge fucking muscles because she thought it looked cool. "It's called 'CrossFit chic'—look it up, sweetie."

She generated new trade routes, established Thebes as a major hub in the world's economy, and ushered Egypt into even more impressive power and prosperity. All in all, she was a fucking fantastic leader. And undeniably she was the most effective estrogen-producing pharaoh to have ever lived. Neither Nefertiti nor Cleopatra even came close to Hatshepsut's level of success. So what ever happened to that stepson?

Well, he slowly grew envious of his stepmom's accomplishments and jealous of what was taken from him. In other words, he fucking hated her. Then, in 1458 BC, Hatshepsut went to heaven (I think she was taken home by aliens), and the twentysomething Thutmose III became pharaoh. His first order of business: erase Hatshepsut from history. He had every statue, monument, painting, and memorial of her completely destroyed, crumbling her legacy to dust so that she would be forgotten and historically denied.

Fortunately for us, modern archaeologists kick ass, and the Egyptians were decent record-keepers. Hatshepsut's mummy was discovered in the early 1900s and positively identified in 2007—and as I write this, her body is currently chilling in Cairo.

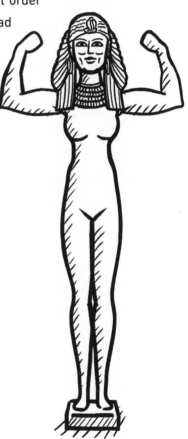

PLAYING WITH DOLLS

There are two ways to handle every breakup: You can move on or you can cling on. The latter makes you assuredly unattractive to anyone else. To illustrate this from both sides, allow me to introduce you to Oskar Kokoschka, famed Austrian artist and poet, and his muse, Alma Mahler.

In 1912, the two met and sparked like flint to steel; Alma quickly became the subject of nearly all Oskar's paintings. However, after three years of mutual obsession, Alma suddenly decided to call it quits—leaving Oskar fucking devastated. So he joined the army in hopes of dying, because a life without Alma wasn't a life he wanted to live. ("Super emo move, dude.") Unfortunately for Oskar and his little emo heart, he survived.

In 1918, still emotionally distraught over Alma, he commissioned a life-size doll to be made in her likeness, hiring a well-known doll maker and providing some disturbingly detailed instructions as to how the doll should be constructed. (Google "Alma Mahler doll" and you'll see just how fucking creepy this thing was.) Although the doll didn't come out as nice as Oskar had hoped, that didn't stop him from parading around town with it, painting portraits of it—eighty to be exact—and doing God knows what with it when the sun went down. Basically, he was as attached to this doll as you are to your phone. Thankfully, Oskar eventually grew tired of the doll (something tells me he wore some holes in it) and threw a big party to celebrate his emotional breakthrough, where he beheaded the doll in front of his guests. ("Wow, another super emo move, dude.") It then took him only twenty-three fucking years to meet another woman. In 1941, he married a nice lady from Prague. If that's not clinging on for far too long, I don't know what is.

So, what happened to Alma during all this? Well, she got on with her life, like any self-respecting individual should. She dated other famous artists, poets, and old-timey celebrities. Essentially, she spent the remainder of her life doing whatever and whomever she wanted. In other words, she handled the breakup the right way.

Now, if you have a friend who is refusing to move on from a past relationship, it's your duty to keep them from becoming Oskar-level gross and pathetic. (Seriously, if your friend starts to create dolls and/or paint pictures of an ex, get them some fucking help—immediately.)

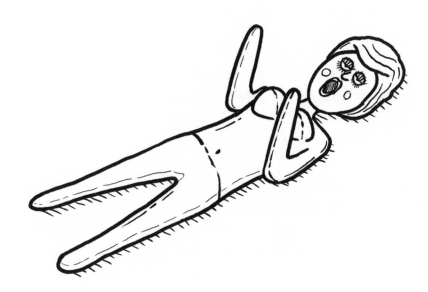

FEAR NOTHING, TAKE EVERYTHING

Hell hath no fury like a woman with nothing to lose. If you drive a strong woman to the point that she no longer gives a fuck, your imagination isn't powerful enough to contemplate the boss that you just unlocked. Take, for example, Queen Boudica of the Iceni, the wife of King Prasutagus.

In AD 43, Claudius of Rome decided to invade the area of Britannia that the Iceni called home. Now, despite being a powerful group, they didn't stand a chance against the armies of Rome, so King Prasutagus surrendered. And for the next seventeen years, the Romans became increasingly controlling. Then, when Prasutagus died in AD 60, the Romans decided to call in all outstanding debts. As part of this, they demanded to take possession of Boudica's estate. She refused. The Romans whipped her, attacked her daughters, and enslaved her royal council . . . leaving her with nothing to lose—oops.

She gathered her remaining supporters and allies to begin a revolt against the Romans. Yes, THE FUCKING ROMANS. Anyone who's ever touched a history book knows that Rome was the predominant world power during this time period, and fucking with Rome was like putting your hand in a pot of boiling water: You're going to get burned. Anyway, like overconfident world powers do, the Romans didn't take Boudica's rebellion seriously and kind of just let it happen, figuring she'd tire herself out. First, she marched on and vanquished the Roman-allied city of Camulodunum. The Romans didn't even respond to this loss. So she decided to go after something the Romans found more valuable: the city of Londinium, the site of modern-day London. There, she showed absolutely no fucking mercy and burned the entire city to the ground. (I don't know what it was with Boudica and fire, but she really liked to burn shit down.) THIS caught the Romans' attention, and the war was on.

Boudica proceeded to attack and burn the city of Verulamium (again with the fucking fire). Okay, now the Romans were pissed. They brought a massive army of chariots to put an end to Boudica's savagery. And they finally did, but not before Boudica's rebellion claimed an estimated seventy thousand to eighty thousand lives over the course of her defiance, making it one of the largest woman-led rebellions in history.

You know what they say about fucking with a bull and getting the horns? Well, fucking with Boudica was clearly a guaranteed way to get burned.

SISTERS STICK TOGETHER

BFF, sister, or partner in crime—it doesn't matter what you call her, every woman has that one friend who's always down for whatever. That friend who forever has your back, that friend who will step in without hesitation to argue on your behalf, and that friend who, if something needs to be handled, will fucking handle it. The two of you are peas in a psychotic pod. No party is too wild, no pizza is too large, and no dick pic is safe from your joint ridicule. Together, you're unstoppable (and fucking hilarious).

Now let's learn about two formidable, history-making BFFs. Allow me to introduce the Tru'ng sisters. Yes, they were actual sisters, but they were also BFFs. (Because sisters stick together, duh.) And together, Tru'ng Trac and Tru'ng Nhi led a rebellion against one of the world's most daunting dynasties: the Han dynasty.

In AD 39, the sisters had finally had enough of China ruling over their homeland of Vietnam, so they assembled an army and put up a fight. And within a year, they were able to take back control of sixty-five settlements. They tag-teamed the Chinese like you and your BFF tag-team an online argument: with focus, determination, and absolute brutality. The sisters amassed an army of nearly eighty thousand—which they commanded by training and appointing thirty-six female generals—making a powerful political statement to fight against a predominantly patriarchal society. To further demonstrate their power, the sisters proclaimed themselves co-queens, and even rode elephants into battle. For three years, the elephant-riding empresses tormented and trampled invading Chinese armies. That is until AD 43 (some sources claim 42), the year the Chinese were finally able to gain the upper hand on the cunning Tru'ngs, defeating them in a battle in what is now Hanoi.

And although it was never proved, it's said that the two sisters took their own lives together, rather than give the Chinese the satisfaction of capturing them. Ride or die.

The next time you and your BFF get together, you should absolutely ride on the backs of elephants. Or maybe just splurge on an upgraded rideshare. (The elephants might be a bit excessive, but it really depends where you live. Plus, in most cases, that's just some touristy bullshit.)

PAINT YOUR OWN PATH

It's nice to have your life figured out, knowing exactly what you want to do, who you want to be, and where you'd like to see yourself in nine years (this number will come back later). But you know what? It's perfectly fine to have no fucking clue what you want to do either. You're looking around and that's cool. Maybe you're still in school "exploring yourself," maybe your options are currently limited given some less-than-ideal life circumstances, or maybe technology just hasn't progressed enough for your dream job to even exist. (I, too, think that being a space veterinarian sounds like a badass profession, but society isn't ready for that yet.)

Now, it goes without saying, the sooner you point your life in the direction of your ultimate goal, the better off you'll be because this will allow you to start mastering your skill set. But don't beat yourself up if you're feeling lost right now; some of history's most prolific contributors were utterly fucking lost at times as well. Take, for example, Vincent Van Gogh—yeah, your grandma has his calendar. He didn't even decide to become a painter until the age of twenty-eight. Before that, Vinnie was just an awkward weirdo who sucked at pretty much anything he attempted, especially dating.

His first love was actually his cousin. Trust me, if you think your love life has been rough, I can assure you that you're doing better than Van Gogh if you've been laid at least once without paying for it. In fact, it was a prostitute who became the recipient of his flesh following his infamous ear incident. He cut off the ear during a manic argument with a friend, but later he gave it to his favorite prostitute as a symbol of his love and affection. My guess: He did this to prove he was a great listener. (He was also a heavy absinthe drinker, so that might have had something to do with it.)

You see, Van Gogh was never able to understand women, but he taught himself to understand watercolors (which are equally as colorful and hard to predict). And although he didn't discover his passion for painting until his late twenties, he created more than two thousand works of art (in various mediums) before his death at age thirty-seven. In nine years, he created a legacy.

Van Gogh was clearly crazy as fuck—you probably shouldn't cut off your ear or fall in love with your cousin—but this story should make you feel a little better about feeling lost while trying to find your path in life.

BLONDES HAVE MORE FUN

Did you know the blonde allele is so recessive and rare that only 2 percent of the world's population has naturally blonde hair? Well, it's true. So throughout the years, those outside the allele in-crowd have tried some pretty weird shit in pursuit of golden locks. Back in the day, you couldn't exactly walk to the store and buy an eight-dollar box of do-it-yourself bullshit. Really, eight dollars? C'mon, of course that product is garbage. If you're trying to go blonde, put up the money to have it done by a professional. You'll be glad you did when you end up looking like an ice princess instead of the fucking pumpkin that was used to make Cinderella's carriage. It's your choice: Do you want to be a princess, or do you want to be a Halloween decoration? While you think about that, let's discuss some old-timey hair-dying techniques.

In ancient Rome, women attained the golden glow with the use of pigeon shit. In Renaissance Venice, they used horse urine. Why? Well, as with most permanent hair dye, both these items contain ammonia. I'm not exactly sure how effective these organic products were (or still are), but what could possibly be more enjoyable than washing your hair with animal excrement? These blondes really were having more fun. And if they weren't, at least their beauty products were made by animals instead of being tested on them, right?

Speaking of blondes having more fun, in ancient

Greece, prostitutes were easy to spot because they usually wore blonde wigs. I guess you could say those blondes were also having more "fun." (However, much like their hair color, they were probably faking it.)

Anyway, don't let anyone tell you that you're a dumb blonde anymore, because you just learned some blonde history. You're welcome.

LEAVE AN IMPRESSION

To further elaborate on the brief mention of Greek prostitution in the previous lesson, do you really think Cinderella was the first girl to purposely leave something behind in order to get a text back? Nope. People have been using that trick for centuries. In fact, the prostitutes of ancient Greece had the art of the leave-behind mastered. They would walk around wearing sandals with the word ΑΚΟΛΟΥΘΕΙ imprinted on the soles. Translation? "Follow me."

As they walked, this message was left behind in the sand for horny Greco-Roman guys. The prostitutes were straight up leaving a trail of foot-made bread crumbs that, if followed, led to an expensive good time. NOTE: Paying for sex is probably the only way a dude wearing flip-flops will ever get laid (we kind of already went over this). So of course prostitution was popular in Greece.

So how does this all apply to you? Simple. Leaving shit behind is a solid dating strategy.

Now, it's worth mentioning that single parents have a major advantage at this game. Because I guarantee, if you leave a kid behind after a first date, you'll definitely be getting a text back to come get him or her—quickly. Hell, you can even use your kid to break the ice with new people as well. It happens like this: You sit down next to an attractive guy or gal at your favorite restaurant, you fake like you're getting an important phone call, then you go outside to "hear better." You casually walk toward your car like you forgot your child and wait for your target to take the bait.

"Oh my God, thank you so much. I can't believe I left my kid behind. I could sure use someone like you in my life. Wanna date?" Yeah, it's that fucking easy.

Don't have kids? Don't worry. If you're creative enough, you can think of a leave-behind equally as effective as a human child. Trust me, I do it all the time. And no, leaving your phone number on the receipt at brunch this weekend in hopes of your server calling you is not a smooth move. Leave something they will actually remember—like a puppy, or your fucking pants.

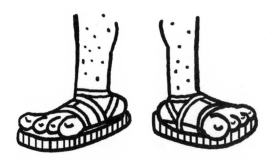

THINK ABOUT IT

Let's be honest here for a minute: You let your imagination get away from you from time to time. It's okay to admit it, because we all do it. We invent scenarios and circumstances that literally have no fucking chance of actually happening. Maybe it's at work, maybe it's at school, or maybe it's within your relationship. (Relax, mermaids and mermen aren't real; there's no fucking way your significant other is cheating on you with a fictional fish skank.) It doesn't matter what area of your life you do this in, the problem with letting your imagination run annoyingly amok is always the same: When you think the worst, you bring out the worst. The worst of your jealousy, the worst of your self-doubt, the worst of your stress, and the worst of your anger.

The good news: Just as easily as your imagination can invent a problem, it can solve a problem. You can use your imagination to overhype things and convince yourself that your significant other is cheating and your cat is plotting to kill you. OR you can use your imagination to create and invent solutions to actual life problems—like the imaginative and badass Maria Beasley did.

In 1884, Maria unveiled one of her creations at an expo in New Orleans: a collapsible lifeboat. The same collapsible lifeboat that, in 1912, would save more than seven hundred people aboard the RMS *Titanic*. Unfortunately, they just didn't have enough of these lifeboats available, or else the outcome of that iceberg collision would have ended differently—because Maria's lifeboats fucking worked. All in all, Maria created and patented a total of fourteen inventions during her lifetime, including a machine that makes wooden wine barrels. Yes, like you, she had an imagination AND a love of intoxication. She just happened to use her imagination and affinity for chardonnay to make a shitload of money instead of a mountain out of a molehill.

So the next time you're drinking wine (you're not alone if the cat's in the room), use your imagination for good instead of paranoid evil—invent something beneficial. Like a wine bottle that's also a stun gun. You know, so you can shock some fucking sense into yourself when you get drunk and start overthinking shit.

THE HEROINES OF HEATING

All great inventions come from a need to solve a problem or a desire to make life more comfortable. At one point in our lives, every one of us has had a great idea for something that we thought would make us millions—but after some thought, we realized that our idea wasn't actually that hot. To illustrate exactly what I mean by "hot," the next two paragraphs are going to talk about a single problem and several solutions that significantly solved it.

The problem: Your girlfriend's hands and feet are fucking freezing. Like all the time. In a room that's a perfect seventy degrees, she bundles up like an Eskimo— how the fuck is that even possible? Well, there are actually biological factors that contribute to why your girlfriend is so much cooler than you (both figuratively and literally): factors like metabolic rate and the specific hormones that vary between men and women. Combined, these create a cool-factor disparity and fuel the battle for thermostat superiority. Trust me, there's science behind the heart of every furious ice queen. Elsa didn't choose to be that way; she was born with the icicle touch. And it's been like this since, well, forever. I bet Eve was giving Adam all sorts of shit about wanting more leaves, but he was too busy gardening or something. (Maybe the snake in the tree simply tempted Eve with a pair of sweet gloves?)

Now, because of this biological difference, nearly every major advance in heating was invented by a frigid female. They had a need, they had a vision, and they took the initiative to heat things up. Let's recap a few of these: The first home with a built-in fireplace was dreamed up and commissioned by Eleanor of Aquitaine during renovations of her French palace sometime around 1137. The first car heater to redirect heat produced by the engine back onto your feet was invented by Margaret A. Wilcox in 1893. The first set of plans for gas-powered central heating was designed by Alice Parker in 1919. The first solar-heated home utilizing a chemical crystallization process to retain heat and radiate it back was built by inventor Maria Telkes in 1947.

So if your girlfriend doesn't return your hoodie, that's just her way of inventing yet another fantastic method of staying warm without your help.

HORSESHOES AND HAND GRENADES

Crossing lines is how you define your life as your own. Your family, society, some random asshole writing on social media—there will always be somebody with an opinion on how you should be living, what you should be doing, and where you should be going. But it's your life, so make the moves that make the most fucking sense to you. For Flora Sandes, the moves that made sense were the moves that were messy, which is exactly why she has such a badass life story.

In 1876, Flora was born in a small English village. Despite her parents' efforts, she preferred things like smoking, fighting, and horseback riding. Growing up, she often said, "I wish I were born a boy." And her desire to do so-called dude shit didn't fade with adulthood. She spent her twenties and thirties traveling and getting into trouble; after she shot a guy in Canada, she decided maybe it was time to return to England. Back home, she joined a nurse organization heading into Serbia to aid in World War I.

There she enlisted with the Red Cross to get closer to the front lines, telling one of the doctors she was working with, "I've always wished to be a soldier and to fight." And in 1915 she got the war opportunity she was wishing for: During Serbia's "Great Retreat" from Albania, all Red Cross workers either fled or were killed—except Flora. As the last woman standing, she was enlisted in the Serbian army, and all her wild childhood hobbies became immediate warfare advantages (good luck being a foodie in a gunfight). She quickly climbed the ranks and was even honored with the Order of Karađorđe's Star. She earned this for a shrapnel injury received during a grenade fight—she won. (Ha, all you'll receive as a foodie is a fucking stomachache.)

Altogether, she earned seven medals and the title Captain Sandes, making her not only the Serbian army's FIRST FEMALE officer but the FIRST FOREIGN officer as well. She retired, got married, authored books, and lectured around the world. In 1956, she died at the age of eighty.

Going forward, anytime you're in need of motivation to live life on your own terms, let Flora be your inspiration. At the very least, maybe she can inspire you to get some cooler hobbies.

(WO)MAN OVERBOARD

Setbacks are a part of life. Sure, some of us will have far more of these than others, both personal and professional. But no matter what happens, you'll survive as long as you continue moving. Whether a failed relationship, a lost job, or a shattered goal, these situations are not the end of the world. Maybe it's a case of bad luck, maybe it's the cause of bad people, or maybe it's the culmination of years of bad decisions—but for the sake of this lesson, let's pretend that luck is all that's pertinent. And let's do this by meeting a woman who, like you, was repeatedly fucked by luck.

Her name was Violet Jessop, and she survived not one, not two, but THREE fucking shipwrecks. (No, not the shipwrecks you consider dating material; we're talking about actual ships—not psychos with dicks.) You see, Violet was a stewardess/nurse who spent her life at sea. In 1911, she was working on the luxurious RMS *Olympic*, which at the time was the largest of its kind. However, proving that size truly doesn't matter, the motion of the ocean took over one day and caused the *Olympic* to collide with another vessel. The good news is that despite suffering significant damage, the ship made it back to port without sinking. Unharmed and without fear, Violet got on with her oceanic career. Her first wreck was kind of like your first serious rejection: not ideal, but nothing too traumatic.

In 1912, Violet was on the RMS *Titanic*. And we all know how that voyage ended, but Violet survived, as she was rescued from lifeboat 16 the morning after that iceberg meeting. "Thanks, Maria Beasley." (Obviously, Jack should have gotten in that boat instead of holding on to Rose's door.) Unrelenting in her love of the ocean, Violet was on the HMHS *Britannic* in 1916 when it sank in the middle of the Aegean Sea following an unconfirmed explosion. Was THIS the end? Nope. Violet jumped out of a lifeboat to avoid being swallowed up by the ship's propeller, and once again, she survived.

At this point, most people would be like, "Fuck this—I'm getting a job at a bank," but not Violet. She wasn't about to let past experiences affect her. She got back to shore and back aboard—not retiring from her seafaring career until 1950.

Now, if Violet's story sounds a bit like your life at the moment, that sucks, but you'll survive. You only sink when you stop swimming.

THE JOKE'S ON THEM

People are going to doubt you. That's just life. But with doubt comes opportunity—the opportunity to prove your doubters wrong—which is truly one of life's greatest pleasures.

Is there anything more satisfying than making someone eat their words by doing exactly what they thought you couldn't do? Let me answer that for you: "No, there isn't." It can be something as major as making a career move or something as minor as eating an entire taco in two bites just to let your date know exactly what they've gotten themselves into.

Regardless of the situation, disproving someone's opinion is always rewarding. You know the feeling I'm talking about, but there's a good chance you don't know the story of Susanna M. Salter. If you do, you're now experiencing the sudden endorphin rush of proving someone (me) wrong—isn't it great? For the rest of you, Susanna, a.k.a. Mayor Salter, was the first woman elected to American political office. The crazy part: She didn't even run. Here's what happened . . .

In 1887, a bunch of dudes put Susanna's name on the ballot for mayor of Argonia, Kansas, hoping the prank would result in such a humiliating loss that it would discourage other women from ever trying to run for office. ("Dumb fucking move, dudes.") But Susanna unknowingly proved those assholes wrong and won, with more than 60 percent of the vote. When news got out, Susanna, only twenty-seven at the time, turned the joke around on them and accepted the position.

And she was fucking great at it, earning the respect of many for her authoritative approach to council meetings. (She handled her meetings like a boss handles an argument: No time for bullshit. Get to the point, or get the fuck out.) When her mayoral term ended, she opted not to run for reelection and moved to Oklahoma, where she lived to be 101 years old. "Ha. Nice try, doc. You were WAY OFF with your forty-year life expectancy of those born in 1860"—yet another thing Susanna was able to disprove during her lifetime. So many good things can come from a desire to discredit others.

There's no need to email me to argue how birth statistics and child mortality rates dramatically decrease life expectancy (especially during the nineteenth century). I already know this, but I also know that 101 is still old as fuck.

SECRECY IS SACRED

Secrets. You can't make friends with 'em; you can't have friends without 'em. There's no better friend than one you can confidently confide in. After all, if you can't trust the people you surround yourself with, what's the fucking point in having them around to begin with?

So what kind of friend are you? Do you keep your friends' news as protected as your own nudes? Or do you treat text messages like a teleprompter and broadcast the contents like a daily weather forecast? "For today's commute, you can expect light rain and a 100 percent chance of Ashley sleeping with her coworker again." You don't need to be a criminal on the run to appreciate and understand the need for keeping certain things between "you and me." On that note, let's travel down south (unless you're already there) to learn about the Mexican War of Independence, the end of Spanish rule, and the contributions of the tight-lipped and tenacious Gertrudis Bocanegra.

Born in 1765 to a Spanish father and a Tarascan Indian mother, Gertrudis grew fluent in several languages and spent much of her time reading, studying, and debating the works of writers, philosophers, and mathematicians. Later in life, she met a dude who shared her views, and the two started a family. In 1810, she was a forty-five-year-old mother to five daughters and two sons when the war officially began. Her husband, Lieutenant de la Vega, and the couple's eldest son joined the resistance while she stayed behind to maintain the family business. Both men were killed. Adamant about continuing their fight—and also about standing up for what she considered to be right—Gertrudis became a messenger to aid her fellow Mexican rebels by delivering confidential communications between commanders.

In 1817, she was captured and tortured, but never revealed a single secretive word. In the end, she was sentenced to death and tied to a tree, where she decided to finally talk, but only to cuss everyone out before being shot. Today in Pátzcuaro, her statue stands in that very spot—now named Plaza Gertrudis Bocanegra.

Gertrudis was the definition of taking secrets to the grave. Remember her story the next time you meet your friends for drinks. And pay close attention to who can actually keep a secret after too many tequila shots—that person should be your best friend.

ONE-SIDED SOBRIETY

Women love wine. And that's cool. It's good to have a hobby. But did you know that in ancient Rome, women were forbidden to drink wine? Yeah. For-fucking-bidden— that's just crazy.

In fact, drinking wine was considered such a serious offense that a man was allowed to divorce his wife if he caught her guzzling the Grigio, chugging the Chianti, swigging the Soave, drinking the . . . okay, I think you get the point. A housewife drinking wine was what the Romans considered a "major fault." Drinking wine ranked right up there with adultery, because the Romans believed drinking wine led to bad decisions . . . like adultery. (FYI: The last known Roman divorce on basis of a "wine-o wifey" was sometime during the second century BC)

First off, duh. Of course drinking wine leads to bad decisions. That's why drinking wine and other intoxicants is good for you: It helps you learn from your mistakes. Second, fuck the Romans. If those guys were so worried that their wives having a drink would lead to cheating, maybe they should have gotten their priorities in order

and stopped being such fucking dicks. And I don't know, maybe hit the gym every once in a while. They could have wrestled with some dudes in the courtyard or something to ensure that they looked like one of those buff-ass statues all over town. There's a reason the Roman women loved watching the sweaty gladiators kill each other: muscles. You think Hercules had to worry about his lady getting drunk and falling on some other dude's cork? No, Hercules was buff as hell. He looked like his dad created him using Photoshop and a chisel.

Anyway, just when you thought you knew everything about wine, you learn something new. I guess even wine snobs can benefit from some history every now and then. You're welcome. Now open a bottle or a box (depending on what your last paycheck looked like), and celebrate your newfound drinking knowledge.

THE MO(U)RNING AFTER

Most of us have been there: Waking up from a night of heavy partying, wondering how you got home, looking for your phone, and beating yourself up for no good reason. Perhaps you're even feeling a bit of unfounded shame; unaware of what you may or may not have done the night before, you're already mentally preparing for the worst. It sucks, right?

Well, if you still have all your hair, it wasn't that bad. Had this happened in fourteenth-century Aztec culture, you'd be looking for a wig AND your dignity. To learn more about this, let's take a fermented field trip to Tenochtitlán. Now the site of modern-day Mexico City, Tenochtitlán was founded as the Aztec religious capital in 1325. And this city-state was home to more than just human sacrifice and sun worship—it was also home to a lot of drunks. (It was like Arizona State University but without all the blonde hair and beer bongs.)

It's well known that the Aztecs were incredibly faithful to their gods, but most people don't know that they were also incredibly forceful with their drinking laws. It seems odd to me that a civilization with religious practices that involved literally bathing the temple steps in human blood would have such harsh punishments for bathing your liver. So just how harsh were these punishments? Well, public intoxication was punishable by death. That is, unless you were attending a festival, or you were over the age of seventy.

Seriously, those were the rules. If you were having organized fun, or you were simply old as fuck, you got a free pass to be a drunk ass. Basically, life six hundred to seven hundred years ago wasn't much different from life today. The Aztecs turned a blind eye to intoxication during celebrations and to certain individuals—much like we do with drug use at music festivals and your grandma's dirty old-lady mouth at family gatherings when she's had a few too many.

Anyway, back to the death penalty for drunken partying: It wasn't something that was used on first-time offenders; it was a punishment reserved for repeated overindulgence. You had to be a serious nuisance to earn that sentence. First-time public drunkards were generally subjected to public ridicule, like property destruction or forcible head shaving. (If you ask me, that might be a fate worse than death because there's no way a skilled barber was doing the shaving.)

Remember this the next time you wake up from a night of getting a little too wasted: As long as you have your phone, hair, and pictures to reflect on, you probably had a good night.

THE SMELL OF VICTORY

Making an entrance is fucking important. Trust me, there's a reason people continually stress the fact that you only get ONE first impression. Pretty much anytime you decide to turn off Netflix and actually go interact with other humans is an opportunity to make a good one. You remember what humans are, right? Of course you do—you've seen them on Netflix.

Anyway, do you want to know who the literal queen of making an entrance was? None other than Cleo-motherfucking-patra. Yeah, she didn't just master winged eyeliner; she mastered pretty much every aspect of sensory seduction. And there's nothing more seductive or memorable than the sense of smell. For example, it's not the sight of a particular alcohol that will make you remember every aspect of your treacherous twenties; it's the smell. Cleopatra knew the nose knows long before scientists were running tests about scent recollection. So before she set out on a diplomatic voyage in 41 BC to meet the Roman general Mark Antony, she made damn sure his nose met her well before he did.

How did she do this? Well, to ensure that she made the best first impression possible, Cleopatra had her ships adorned with beautiful purple sails that were absolutely fucking soaked in her favorite perfume prior to setting off. Thus, the same winds that would carry her boats to Rome would also carry the scent of her perfume to the shore before her arrival. Goddamn, say what you want about Cleopatra being a crazy snake lady, but she basically invented the art of arriving fashionably late. I mean, when your scent gets there before you do, you're setting quite the stage for yourself.

And, well, it fucking worked. After catching wind of Cleo's arrival, Mark was head over heels for her days before her feet even touched Roman soil, and the two quickly became lovers and allies—forming the original "power couple."

So the next time somebody tells you that you're wearing too much perfume, tell 'em you're just allowing your reputation to precede you.

THINK FAST AND YOUR
LEGEND MIGHT LAST

One quick reaction can easily become your new reputation, defining your life for years to come. It's a weird yet beautiful thing how a spur-of-the-moment decision can take two distinctly different routes. Just as quickly as you can do something that makes you appear unstable and crazy, you can do something else that makes you utterly incredible. One day you're sending psychopathic texts to your ex; and the next, your fast hands, lack of personal concern, and insanely quick response time might actually save someone's life. Your instincts can lead you in so many different directions from day to day, which can be an overwhelming and scary thought, but not second-guessing yourself in times of crisis can, and will, pay off. You don't think; you just act—like Pancha Carrasco did in the 1850s. You've probably never heard of her, so let me hit you with a bit of backstory.

Born in Costa Rica in 1816 (not '26; her name change seems to confuse some), she lived a rather quiet life until the year 1856. It was then that her quick thinking and no-fucks-given attitude made her a Costa Rican sensation and historic icon.

While she was volunteering as an army cook and medic during the Second Battle of Rivas, the camp in which she was living and working was attacked. She could have easily fled (some of the men did), but instead she found a rifle and filled the pockets of her apron with bullets. (Guys, this is why your girlfriend is obsessed with any dress that has pockets. She's ready to hold anything: phone, snacks, bullets—you name it. On second thought, this makes much more sense than using your armpit to hold things—like we discussed earlier on page twenty-two.) Equipped with her weapon and warfare wardrobe, Pancha joined the front lines, becoming the first woman ever to fight in the Costa Rican military. Her quick reaction became a symbol of national pride, and forever after, her reputation was that of female ferocity. She's had her name emblazoned across a military ship and her face placed on a postage stamp, and her legacy inspired the Costa Rican Pancha Carrasco Police Women's Excellence Award.

In conclusion, here's a challenge: Live a little more like Pancha, and don't second-guess yourself for the next twenty-four hours—just act and see what happens. Maybe you'll end up on a stamp, maybe you'll end up in the back of a squad car. Either way, just think of how cool it will be to tell your grandchildren the story someday.

A STABBY STANDOFF

Defend what's yours. Your girl, your man, your opinion—if you feel passionate about ANYTHING, by all means defend it. When somebody insults your boyfriend or girl-friend, you'd better step up and shut that shit down. When somebody tells you that you're wrong, don't be timid but stand by your opinion. And when somebody reaches across the table to snag a fry from your plate without asking, put a fork between their third and fourth metacarpal. (If it's a first date and you hope to land a second, maybe try a wrist slap instead of a hand stab. You don't want to come off too crazy too quickly—we still live in a civilized society.) Okay, all french-fry fork-play aside, you get what I'm saying: If you care about something, defend it and fight for it, re-gardless of how overwhelmed, outnumbered, or unprepared you might be.

Speaking of fighting, let's go back a few hundred years and learn something. The year is 1797 and the French have just invaded Wales, triggering the Battle of Fish-guard, a short-lived conflict, thanks to heavy opposition from everyday Welsh civil-ians not about to let French intruders call their city home. One such civilian's actions were the very definition of defending what's yours.

Her name was Jemima Nicholas, and she took it upon herself to get these foreign fucks out of her town. So one night she ventured out and came across a group of French soldiers in the midst of an invasion celebration. (What's more annoying than uninvited guests? Uninvited guests throwing a fucking party.) Armed with nothing but a pitchfork—and outnumbered twelve to one—Jemima disturbed, disarmed, and detained all these would-be partygoers inside the local church.

The following morning, all twelve soldiers surrendered to the British army, and

Jemima's heroic actions are forever marked on her gravestone outside St. Mary's Church in Fishguard, Wales.

Huh, looks like forks are just as effective at defending against French invaders as they are at defending a plate of french fries from an aggressive first-dater. So when the time comes, put down this book, pick up a fork, and prepare to defend what's yours.

BATHING IN BELIEVABILITY

Do what you say you're going to do, be where you say you're going to be, and never make a promise you don't intend to keep. Your word is your most valuable possession. Be like Queen Tomyris and always keep your word. Let's learn more about her extreme example of commitment.

In 530 BC, Queen Tomyris (ruler of the Massagetae, eastern Iranian nomads) clashed with the Persian conqueror Cyrus the Great on land that is now Kazakhstan. Thinking he could make quick work of the Massagetae, Cyrus offered to marry Tomyris as a means of avoiding the battle altogether. She declined. (Good move. It sounds like he wasn't really in it for the right reasons—like an old-timey version of *The Bachelor* or some shit.) Disgruntled, Cyrus retreated, but not before leaving a small group behind in a camp stocked full of intoxicants. And, well, Tomyris's armies fell for it: They raided the camp, killed the men left behind, and got completely trashed in false celebration of defeating the Persians—Cyrus's plan all along.

Then, taking advantage of their inebriation, Cyrus's armies returned, killed a ton, and kidnapped Tomyris's son. In retaliation, Tomyris sent Cyrus a letter calling him a bloodthirsty bitch and challenged him to a rematch, vowing to give him more blood than he could ever drink in a lifetime. He accepted, but this time Tomyris and her armies were ready and defeated the Persian invaders. Cyrus himself was killed and his body brought to Tomyris; she proceeded to cut off his head and repeatedly dunk it in a basin of blood.

Yep, true to her word, she gave him more blood than his life could handle. After which she made his skull into a souvenir cup to use for quenching her own thirst, a customary practice among her people. I imagine her skull mug looked like a spooky Halloween decoration from Target—except way more realistic.

Obviously, this is an extreme example of keeping your word, but the next time you make plans to meet for drinks, be there, be reliable—be the one who's always on time and already three drinks ahead.

BLOOD OF YOUR ENEMIES

SEAFARING SISTERS

Like-minded people make living infinitely more enjoyable. You need AT LEAST one person in your life who shares your same likes, dislikes, aspirations, attitude, and outlook. You know, someone who's just as weird and ridiculous as you and will ride life's crazy waves with you. This could be a friend, or this could be a lover; whoever it is, there's no denying they make your life better. And while we're still on the topic of crazy waves, let's talk about two infamous sea women. No, not mermaids; these foulmouthed harlots were fucking pirates. Their names were Anne Bonny and Mary Read, and they were virtually inseparable.

The duo first met in 1718 and quickly bonded over a shared secret: They were each posing as a man in order to more readily climb the buccaneer ranks. In addition to this, they also shared a quick temper, a disdain for ordinary life, and a love of conflict. After revealing themselves as women, the pair earned the nickname "hellcats" because they wielded their pistols (and their pussies) with lionlike ferocity. For example, Mary once killed a crewmember for attempting to start a duel with the dude she was currently banging. And, well, when Anne's husband (also a pirate) was found guilty of piracy and sentenced to death, she simply said, "Had you fought like a man, you need not have been hanged like a dog." It's easy to see why these two nutjobs were best friends, right?

Anyway, in 1720 their ship was captured by the British navy, and being inseparable, they were tried together in court—becoming the first two women in European history to be legally convicted of piracy. However, they both avoided the death penalty because they were both pregnant. (Seriously, they did EVERYTHING together.)

After this, records vary as to what happened, but most likely Mary died in prison, and Anne returned to pirate life under a different name after a wealthy relative purchased her freedom.

Now, as quickly as Anne and Mary's good times on the high seas came to an end, your good times can begin. Text the person you were thinking about when I introduced this story to see how down they are for quitting their job and buying a boat.

GEOLOGICAL CALL GIRLS

Okay, this history isn't as old as the history you'll find in the rest of this book, but it happened in the 1990s, and, well, that decade is still fucking history. Plus, the penguin discussion in the following paragraphs is just as interesting and applicable to your life as the stories of people found in the others. Think of this as a timely break to talk about beaks. (Because I like birds.) Finding your "penguin" is a stupid dream. Why? Because penguins are cheaters—some of them are even prostitutes. (Surprising for an animal that always wears a tuxedo.)

I know it's rough accepting the fact that everyone in your life has lied to you about penguin monogamy, but it's not nearly as rough as penguins like it. So let's learn more about these feathery little fuck-buddies. For this, we travel to the year 1998. The year Fiona Hunter, a researcher at the University of Cambridge, concluded her five-year study of Adélie penguins. Also the same year that a US president denied having sexual relations with an intern. Coincidence? I think not. Anyway, while studying the birds' mating habits, Dr. Hunter noticed that some females would wander off when their mate was out hunting for food. Why? Duh, to have sex with the male penguins who stayed behind—it was like an episode of *Desperate Housewives* filmed on a fucking beach. After doing the dirty bird, the female would take a stone from the male's nest as payment. (For penguins, stones are like shoes: You can never have too many.)

But the females weren't doing this just to get their nesting rocks off; they were doing this to test out future mates. You know, so they'd have a replacement in case their husband was eaten by a killer whale or some shit. Basically, the Adélie females were using sex to get what they wanted. Females were even observed tricking the males by assuming the position. Then when the male got all dumb and excited over the thought of getting laid, she'd grab a stone from his nest and fucking jet. Ha. Like a hooker stealing a dude's wallet. I love it.

So there you have it: If your goal is a cute, monogamous relationship, don't choose a penguin as your spirit animal. But if your goal is to be a fucking man-eater, by all means, BE A FUCKING PENGUIN. And the next time your boyfriend calls you his penguin, respond with, "Who the fuck are you calling a prostitute?! You don't pay me for this shit, but you should."

ASHLEY'S FAKE EYELASHES

Jealousy. It's a hell of a thing. There is literally no other human emotion quite like it. It's powerful, it's sickening, and it causes people to do some ridiculous shit. Destroyed marriages, broken friendships, shattered careers—people will completely fuck up their lives over stupid feelings of envy, anxiety, and resentment. Guys are jealous of another guy's car, girls are jealous of another girl's guy, and everybody is jealous of somebody with great eyes and eyelashes. Yeah, you heard me. Don't act like you don't wish your eyes were fucking pretty. Yes, even you, Mr. Macho Man. You know you'd blink the shit out of Paul Walker eyes if you had them (RIP).

People say eyes are the window to the soul, but that's some bullshit. Eyes are more like the doorway to your dreams. Seriously, if you have a sweet set of peepers—and you know how to use them—you can pretty much write your ticket in life. You can brainwash people with your baby blues and get yourself into all sorts of fun and/or trouble. You can even bounce from bedroom to bedroom if you're into that sort of thing, because everybody wants to have sex with a pretty-eyed stranger.

Speaking of sexy eyes, the ancient Romans believed eyes—in particular, the eyelashes—were directly related to how much sex a person was having. Long eyelashes? She's a good, wholesome gal saving herself for marriage. Short, thin, ragged eyelashes? You better believe that girl is homie hopping. In fact, Pliny the Elder once said, "Eyelashes fall out from excessive sex, and so it is especially important for women to keep their eyelashes long to prove their chastity." Ha, now that's some bullshit. However, it was this belief that contributed to the invention of fake eyelashes and eye makeup. Yep, filters for your face and eyelids have been around since ancient Roman times.

Well, there you have it. Now you know why your friend Ashley refuses to leave the house without her fake eyelashes—she's just trying to look like Roman marriage material. "Lookin' good, Ash."

A PIRATEY PROPOSAL

People will treat you the way you allow them to treat you. If you want to be respected, you have to first respect yourself. Draw the line on what you deem acceptable; stand up, speak out, and shut shit down when you don't like a situation. You might think the phrase "fortune favors the brave" is simply a reference to adventurous sexual positions, and it is. But it applies to every other aspect of your life as well. Specifically those times when you need to set the tone for permissible conduct.

Born in 1661, Anne Dieu-le-Veut knew what she wanted and wasn't afraid to kiss, kill, or steal for it. This was an attitude that led to a life of crime and eventually her deportation from mainland France to the island of Tortuga with the rest of the criminal castaways. There, in 1684, she met and married Pierre Lelong, a corsair who showed her the ropes of the rebellious pirate lifestyle. Together, they pillaged and plundered for six years, until piracy caught up to Pierre and he was killed in a fight in 1690.

In 1691, Anne once again tried the marriage thing, having a short-lived piratey fling with Joseph Cherel. Unfortunately, in 1693 Cherel was also killed in a fight. But on this night, Anne found out who killed him because the killer quickly made insulting remarks to her following the ordeal. Now, killing her husband was one thing (all part of a pirate's life), but directly insulting her? No, no, no—not fucking cool. So she challenged him to a duel. But he wasn't just some random guy at the bar; he was Laurens de Graaf, one of the most feared pirate captains of the time and rumored by many to be the devil himself (he sounds handsome).

After further humiliating her, de Graaf drew his sword, and, well, Anne drew her pistol. Impressed with her show of force—and probably also realizing he was about to be shot to shit—de Graaf promptly asked Anne to marry him. She accepted. And just like that, the most powerful pirate couple of the seventeenth century was formed; definitely a "How did you meet?" story worth telling the grandkids.

Anyway, the next time you're on a date, if you don't like what someone has to say, make them pay—for your drinks or with their life.

FOCUS ON FINISHING

Longevity is the key to accomplishing damn near anything. Think about the New Year's resolutions you set for yourself every January; how long does it take before you give up and your new goals, again, become next year's resolutions? I get it—it's easy to become distracted and forget why you even made those ridiculous resolutions in the first place. (Seriously, who the fuck wants to exercise every day anyway?) But like most goals, nothing worth having comes easily—not a revenge body, not sobriety, and definitely not the dignity that comes from keeping your text-happy fingers under control when you're drunk, lonely, and missing somebody.

If you want to avoid setting the same resolutions year after year, keep your eye on the fucking prize. Like one young man did back in sixth-century Greece, during a time when Cleisthenes, king of Sicyon, put a dozen suitors through a grueling yearlong competition for the ultimate reward: a blessing of marriage to his daughter, Agariste. (Yes, you read that correctly: AN ENTIRE FUCKING YEAR. No way your ex would have done that. He couldn't get off social media long enough to give you even five minutes of undivided attention, let alone spend 365 days participating in a grueling competition that was basically the ancient equivalent of *The Bachelorette*.)

Wrestling, chariot races, musical performances—nothing was off limits during this twelve-month free-for-all for the hand of the heiress to the throne. It's worth understanding that whoever married Agariste would also someday take the Sicyon throne. So yeah, this contest doubled as a job interview to find a man with the tenacity necessary to rule a kingdom. After a year, only two men remained: Megacles of the powerful Alcmaeonidae family, and Hippocleides, just some handsome-ass Athenian guy—kidding, this dude's family was also fucking loaded.

On the final night, during a dinner to conclude the yearlong competition and announce the winner, Hippocleides got super fucking drunk and danced around like an idiot. So Cleisthenes instantly declared Megacles the winner, proving just how important it is to stay focused on your goals until the end. Who knows? Hippocleides may have had it in the bag if he could have resisted cheese, wine, and slags.

If you're ever tempted to give in or celebrate too early, think back on this story. Also feel free to plan a year's worth of competitive activities for anyone looking to date you. Invite them all to the same bar, have them sign disclosures, then LET THE FUCKING GAMES BEGIN. (This way, at least everybody is aware they're playing.)

THE LUNATIC OF LITERATURE

Renegades rule the world. Those who aren't afraid to be uncomfortable, those who aren't afraid to speak out, and, well, those who aren't afraid to appear downright fucking crazy from time to time. Basically the kind of person Nellie Bly was during her fifty-seven years on this weird rock we humans call home.

Born May 5, 1864, as Elizabeth Jane Cochran, young Liz was never one to shy away from confrontation. In 1885, after reading an article that implied women were basically just baby factories, twenty-year-old Liz wrote a fuck-off style letter to the editor. Impressed by her response, he offered her a job, and she began writing under the pseudonym Nellie Bly. After years of being stuck writing articles on topics that she thought sucked, she took a job as an investigative journalist and sought to uncover the mistreatment of patients at the Women's Lunatic Asylum on what is now Roosevelt Island in New York City. How? By becoming a patient.

She spent a few hours staring in the mirror—practicing making crazy eyes and animal faces (like experimenting with social media face filters)—then she checked herself into a boardinghouse. There, she flipped her crazy switch to the "ON" position and waited for management to pay attention. It worked. She was taken in for an examination, and a group of doctors deemed her insane—committing her to the asylum. But not before she caught the eye of local media, which dubbed her "pretty crazy girl" in a newspaper article.

She spent ten days dealing with ice baths, shitty food, and forced restraint before her publisher stepped in to convince the asylum she was undercover and not actually unhinged. After this, Nellie wrote the book *Ten Days in a Mad-House*, garnering worldwide acclaim and forcing the so-called experts to explain how she'd tricked them (which also prompted an investigation into the asylum itself). Then Nellie went on to further challenge society by traveling around the world in seventy-two days just to prove the Jules Verne book *Around the World in Eighty Days* wrong.

Crazy? Debatable. Badass? Definitely.

Now, ladies, if a man ever calls you a lunatic, respond with, "This is totally going in my book," and watch him fucking panic with confusion.

KEEP YOUR HEAD

Trophy wife, trophy husband, trophy girlfriend, and so on—why the fuck would any-body want to be a trophy? Sure, it's cool to be with someone who's proud to have you. But by definition, a trophy is simply "a cup or decorative object awarded for victory or success." Fuck that. Your life is meant to be a series of rewards you earn for yourself, not a reward for somebody else.

Here's the point where someone says, "But, Captain, being called a 'trophy' means you're rare and highly prized." Pfft, no it doesn't. A Starbucks cup can be considered a trophy: It's a cup, it has the recipient's name on it, it's a reward for doing something difficult—like actually getting out of bed before noon—and it (oftentimes) requires braving long lines and sacrifice.

Sounds like a trophy if you ask me. (Albeit, more along the lines of a participation trophy, since everyone and their dog can get one.) My point in all this: Don't strive to be a trophy on somebody else's shelf of life; strive to be feared and respected—live life like Nakano Takeko.

Born in 1847, Nakano was taught samurai combat from her adoptive father at a young age. So in 1868, it was no surprise that she chose to lead a guerrilla army of female samurai during the Boshin War, also known as the Japanese Revolution. Although this she-devil (a nickname we discussed earlier) samurai squad wasn't a sanctioned army regiment, its members were just as feared as their male counter-parts, proving you don't need a meat sword to be fucking scary. As the leader, Na-kano knew she was number one on the imperial hit list, so she instructed her sister, Yuko, to cut off her head and bury it if she were ever killed to prevent anyone from keeping her skull as a trophy (a customary practice with old-timey warfare).

And it happened: Nakano was shot and killed during a battle in Ogaki. True to her word, Yuko removed her sister's head and buried it under a tree. At this spot now stands the Nakano Takeko Monument in Aizubange, Fukushima, Japan.

Now that you've finished reading this, take a break from this book, get some coffee, and go cut off some heads. Not literally; that's some straight-up serial-killer shit that will land you in prison—definitely not a place you want to be considered somebody's trophy.

NO CHILD, THANKS TO CROCODILES

Let's be honest, condoms suck. Nobody likes them. Not your mom, not your dad, not even the lady in your building living in 6E. (Yes, even Carol hates getting it with the use of a dick mitten.) But sadly enough, condoms work. They keep your junk from burning, your crotch from itching, and, most importantly, your life from falling apart. Because unless you're absolutely ready for it, pregnancy can be a soul-crushing experience.

Accordingly, people have been finding ways to avoid the destructive nature of children long before the invention of the weenie glove. Even as far back as 1850 BC, a time when the ancient Egyptians got rather creative and resourceful with crocodiles. Yes, crocodiles. Toothy, reptilian, ferocious creatures—you know, like your boyfriend's ex-girlfriend. And with anywhere from sixty to seventy-two teeth and a four-thousand-pound bite force, I would imagine putting your dick in a crocodile's mouth is pretty fucking awful. Call me crazy, but I don't think a blowjob should feel like going on a safari.

Anyway, the ancient Egyptians made good use of the plentiful Nile crocs when it came to keeping a baby out of your lady box. So how exactly did the Egyptians use the crocodiles? Well, it's actually quite simple. (Fucking gross, but simple.) They mixed crocodile dung, mud, and honey together to create an all-natural, highly effective spermicide. The pH level of crocodile dung will pretty much kill any little swimmer trying to find a home. First, I don't even want to know how the fuck the Egyptians figured that out. Second, the first lady to volunteer to cover her vagina in crocodile shit, mud, and honey must have been into some seriously kinky stuff.

Now remember, pregnancy is never a good game plan to lock down a guy. In fact, you shouldn't let any guy wearing cargo shorts even near your lady parts. (That's probably the easiest way to avoid getting pregnant because it automatically eliminates 99 percent of all men.) But the 1 percent of men without cargo shorts might be worth risking it. Because they're most likely doctors or have some other career that requires them to respect themselves.

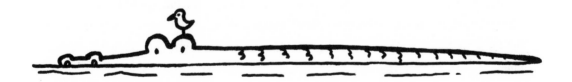

THE DENTIST OF DEATH

Alfred Southwick: steamboat engineer, mechanic, inventor, and dentist. Yeah, a dentist—what kind of sick fuck wants to be a dentist? Well, I'm about to tell you . . .

Now, Alfred wasn't just your average dentist, because if he were, you wouldn't be reading about him today. You see, Alfred didn't just pull teeth and play with his pick all day; Alfred was the dude who invented the electric chair. I mean, who other than a dentist would invent a chair that fucking kills you? Hell, the last time I went to the dentist, I wish someone would have killed me.

Born in 1826, Alfred always had a knack for mechanical mischief. Shortly after graduating high school in Ohio, he moved to Buffalo, New York, where he began inventing dental tools. Again, who the fuck just wakes up one day and ponders, "Huh, you know what this world needs? More dental tools." God, this dude just keeps getting weirder and weirder.

Anyway, after successfully completing a dental apprenticeship at the not-so-young age of thirty-six, Alfred became a dentist himself and opened his own practice. It was here that he perfected the art of strapping people to chairs and putting strange objects in their mouths. However, it wasn't until the year 1881 that Alfred got the idea for the electric chair. After hearing about some dumbass drunk dude accidentally electrocuting himself to death, Alfred became intrigued by electricity and its deadly potential. (George was the name of the drunk dude who electrocuted himself, in case you were wondering.) Most people would hear that story and be like, "Oh shit, that's fucking . . . sad," but not Alfred. Alfred was like, "Oh shit, that's way cooler than cavities." So as a former mechanic, Alfred got to work.

By 1888, he had the first electric chair prototype ready for action. And on January 1, 1889, the first law allowing death by means of electrocution went into effect in New York State.

So the next time you're brushing your teeth with that electric toothbrush your dentist recommended, just know that if Alfred were still alive today, he'd probably find a way to make that toothbrush electrocute you to death.

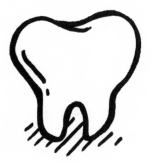

ALL OF THE ABOVE

Life is not black and white, this or that, or one direction versus the other. Just because you're one thing, doesn't mean you can't also be another. Here's what I mean by that: You can (and should) be a multifaceted individual. Be someone with contrasting hobbies, varying interests, and a diversity of passions that keeps people guessing. Blur the lines on what people expect of you, like Julie D'Aubigny did in seventeenth-century France.

Born around 1670, Julie was the daughter of a noble who served under King Louis XIV; and as such, she had to deal with some royal bullshit—like an arranged marriage to Count Maupin. Fortunately, her so-called husband was always gone, allowing Julie to pursue a range of interests and, well, physical activities. She met a fencing master who taught her how to fight, she had a love affair with a nun—even burned down the convent so the two could run away together—and she decided dressing like a dude was more fun. She also took up dueling as her preferred method of solving conflict, killing or injuring nearly a dozen men this way. Alas, this was not enough.

So in 1690, she decided to take a stab at other things, namely the Paris Opera. Using the name Mademoiselle de Maupin, she was magnificent and in 1701 was dubbed "the most beautiful voice in the world." Despite her singing success, she never fully left her stabby ways behind. And one night, upon overhearing a male counterpart talking shit about some of the female performers, she confronted him on the street and challenged the mouthy monsieur to a duel. He refused to fight a woman, so she beat his ass with a cane and took his watch (not returning it until he publicly begged her).

Okay, let's recount this real quick: She was a royal, an opera singer, a cross-dresser, a nun lover, a swordfighter, and pretty much an all-around badass—it's too bad she died in 1707, because God only knows what cool fucking thing she would have become next (hopefully not a DJ).

Now, who said you have to be the same person today that you were yesterday? I think it's time you found another hobby.

SET YOUR SIGHTS ON SUCCESS

Your age might create doubt, your background can cause hesitation, and your gender may be met with skepticism. Because let's be honest, no matter where you come from, who you are, or what you're into, someone is going to think less of you because of it. Maybe your boss doesn't believe you're right for the promotion, maybe your date doesn't think you can finish that entire entrée by yourself (Chad clearly doesn't fucking know who he matched with), or maybe even your own family doubts the strength of your ambition. But you know what? Fuck all that. Let's meet someone who was the epitome of rebellion in motion.

Her name was Roza Shanina—I know, reminds me of Shania Twain too—but Roza wasn't an award-winning singer-songwriter; she was a medal-decorated Soviet soldier. Born April 3, 1924, in a small Russian village, Roza was one of six children and by far the most outspoken, opinionated, and, you guessed it, utterly fucking rebellious. At the age of fourteen, despite her parents' disapproval, she hiked 120 miles to the nearest railroad station to catch a train and enroll in college. (And you thought your 9:00 a.m. class across campus was "too much.")

She graduated in 1941, during the middle of World War II—a war that had just claimed the life of her brother. So what does a fucking unstoppable seventeen-year-old with a college degree do? She volunteers for the draft, of course. She was denied but continued to submit applications until, in 1943, she was accepted to sniper school. (Fun fact: Soviets chose to enlist females as snipers because they believed women were more calculating, cunning, and patient than men. This is true. And also the reason why your girlfriend wins most arguments.)

In 1944, Roza was shot but later wrote in her diary, "I didn't feel it." (Yeah, she was the real OG of ignoring feelings.) She went on to become one of the Soviet Union's most successful snipers before being killed at the age of twenty while shielding her wounded commander. For this, she was awarded the Medal for Courage, and several monuments and memorials have appeared throughout the years in her honor.

If you constantly hear the word "no," be like Roza—get on a train and fucking go.

TRUST YOUR GUT

Chances are, you've been told to trust your gut more than once in life. It doesn't matter who it came from—advice from a parent or advice from a friend. In the end, what matters is whether you trust yourself enough to actually fucking do it. (No, I'm not talking about refusing to apologize for the awful things you say when you're hungry; that's an entirely different type of abdominal confidence.) But trust *me* when I say this: You'll regret the times you don't side with your intuition far more than you will the times you choose to roll the dice on your inner sense of direction. Additionally, if you can't trust yourself, who are you to believe others should ever put their trust in you? If you want to become someone who's relied upon, learn to trust yourself more than anyone.

Speaking of risky reliance, can you think of anything that requires you to trust your gut instincts more than military warfare? I mean, on the battlefield, nearly every choice is literal life or death. For fuck's sake, your decisions are easy compared with this. (You've been dating for only three weeks; people have cold sores longer than that.) Okay, enough talk, let's meet Lozen, Apache warrior and medicine woman.

Born in the 1840s, during the American Indian Wars, Lozen was as cunning as she was confident, as astute as she was ardent, and definitely as dreaded as she was dependable. Why? Because she trusted her gut, and subsequently people trusted her. In fact, many believed she had powers of premonition that aided her, like she was a predator hunting prey. Thus, her instincts were enlisted to lead the majority of Apache warfare initiatives. Her foresight, combined with a willingness to get her hands dirty, made her a force to be reckoned with. She saved women from imprisonment, rescued infants from reservations, and once even slaughtered a steer with a knife to avoid giving away her location. She was a savior and a warrior.

In 1885 she joined the legendary Geronimo in the final stand of the Apache Wars, leading to her imprisonment. Then, unfortunately, the other thing she couldn't see coming: tuberculosis. (Which took her life in 1889.)

If you ever have a sick feeling that you're onto something, trust your intuition and get rid of whatever it is the same way that you would an embarrassing lip abrasion: as quickly as possible.

FLIPPING THE BIRD

In life there will be a time when the world's ways are against you. But here's the deal: The world can get to you only if you choose to be of this world. Now, I know what you're thinking, "There he goes, talking about aliens again." For once, I'm not. What I'm saying is that you can either accept everything the way it is—allowing the world's current ways to win—or you can say, "Fuuuck this," and find your own way, putting bullshit barriers behind you instead of letting them get the best of you. You'll have to leave behind self-doubt, failed routes, and even those people who aren't working out. "Sorry, Carrie, but you're not good for my self-care."

Essentially, move beyond anything and everything that gets in your fucking way. In Bessie Coleman's case, that impediment was an entire continent. In 1892 in a rural Texas town, Bessie became the tenth of thirteen children born to opportunistic sharecroppers. Early on, life didn't seem too promising; it was composed of mostly farming, occasional schooling, and a lot of moving. Then, at the age of twenty-four (while working as a manicurist in Chicago), she overheard the stories of pilots returning from World War I, piquing her own aerial ambitions. The problem: No flight school would accept her application. So what did Bessie do? She taught herself French and moved to, well, motherfucking France.

There, she attended the Caudron Brothers' School of Aviation and became the first-ever African American woman to earn her pilot's license. In 1922, she became the first-ever African American woman to pilot a commercial flight. But commercial flights were too boring for Bessie, so she became a stunt pilot, performing under the moniker Queen Bess—parachuting her way into the public eye with feats of brazen aviation. She drew crowds of thousands to her performances. Sadly, it was at one of these awe-inspiring performances that a failed stunt took her life in 1926. But not before she effectively broke through all sorts of barriers during her brief thirty-four years on Earth.

Barriers are not impassable. If you can't get around them, do like Queen Bess did and fly over the top of them. (Even cooler if you also complete a flip while doing it.)

LIFE'S LITTLE CHANGES

Life enhancements don't always require large, grandiose actions. In fact, it's the small tweaks that can often lead to the most significant of things. Take, for example, brushing your teeth. It doesn't require much to fill your mouth with some bristles, but doing so will dramatically affect whether somebody is willing to kiss you. And a simple kiss can lead to so much more—like a relationship, everlasting love, or a cold sore. But no matter what, mighty or minuscule, the one thing that nearly all choices (and cold sores) have in common is this: Other people will have questions. Humans love having opinions, either positive or negative. Your actions—and more importantly, your choices—will be especially questioned by those who believe they know better. Even when your choice seems like a relative no-brainer. Because, well, common sense doesn't always prevail, and we, as humans, are always learning.

In the nineteenth century (and pretty much every previous century) childbirth was an incredibly risky undertaking. Expectant mothers were susceptible to a variety of complications, including puerperal fever, a.k.a. "childbed fever," a postpartum in-fection of the reproductive system due to less-than-sanitary birthing conditions. So after seeing this happen time and time again in his own obstetrics practice, Dr. Ignaz Semmelweis decided to do something about it. The Hungarian-born surgeon, physi-cian, and scientist proposed a radical new idea: Let's wash our fucking hands before venturing into babyland.

Dr. Semmelweis simply suggested that physicians use a sterilizing or bleaching agent on their hands prior to delivery. But his handwashing hypothesis was met with extensive criticism from his obstetrical peers and the scientific powers that be (seriously, science nerds won't believe a damn thing without numbers and verifiable evidence—kind of like a jealous, toxic ex).

Regardless, Dr. Semmelweis made the change in his own operations while working at the Vienna General Hospital in Austria. And despite a drastic reduction in infections and ultimately the mortality rates of his female patients, he was largely ostracized for the remainder of his medical career. So much so that in 1865 he was committed to a mental asylum by his former colleague, where he was badly beaten by the guards upon arrival. Subsequently, DUE TO AN UNSANITARY ENVIRONMENT, he died fourteen days later from an infection caused by the incident. He was only forty-seven.

Years later, Dr. Semmelweis's ideas were acknowledged and deemed necessary after the French chemist Louis Pasteur published his findings on germ theory, proving that, yeah, washing your hands is a good fucking idea. So the next time you're in the process of suggesting something new, trying something new, or becoming someone new, remember that not everyone is going to get it, accept it, or support it, but that doesn't mean you're not doing the right shit.

A MATHEMATICAL MATRIARCH

In a world of vanity, knowledge is the best form of mutiny. While everyone else is focused on their looks, rebel and bury your face within a fucking book. (This book is a decent start.)

Here's the deal: At some point, you're probably going to get ugly—not everyone is destined to age gracefully—but your knowledge will always stay with you. Like an incurable STD, knowledge can be passed around but never truly passed off. And when you share it, you can do some incredibly cool shit with it. Like the French mathematician, author, physicist, philosopher, AND gambler Émilie du Châtelet did during the eighteenth century.

Born in 1706, Émilie was a bit of a daddy's girl, which proved to be beneficial, since her father was quite influential. Early on, he supported Émilie's academic ambitions by arranging one-on-one tutoring sessions with the best minds and mentors he could find. By the age of twelve, Émilie was fluent in five languages and exceptionally efficient in math and science. So much so that her mother feared she was becoming too smart and tried to have Émilie sent to a convent—didn't happen. ("Mom, my brain is nun of your fucking business.") Like a true rebel, Émilie used her math skills to pay the bills by mastering card games and spending her winnings to further her learning.

In 1737, Émilie wrote a paper regarding heat and light, explaining what we now know as infrared radiation. In 1738, this paper was published, making her the first woman ever to have a scientific article recognized by the Paris Academy of Sciences. In 1740, she released her first book, titled *Lessons in Physics*. In 1747, she wrote a book on mathematics that contradicted the equations previously set forth by French astronomers (she was right). In 1749, thanks to her language skills, she completed a full translation of Newton's *Principia*, eventually spurring a scientific revolution in France. Sadly, that same year she died of complications from childbirth. (Ugh, kids ruin everything.)

Now, I know math isn't always fun, but you can hone your skills by taking full advantage of happy-hour drink specials. (Don't forget to carry more than one drink at a time and factor "hours remaining" into your estimated total hangover level.)

FAME AND FORTUNE

A normal life is not for everyone. You ever have that underlying feeling that you were meant for something more—like you were destined to make a difference? Good, it's those with a defined life direction who end up leaving the most indelible impressions.

Born in 1721, Jeanne-Antoinette Poisson wasn't just another Parisian princess. In fact, she wasn't a princess at all. But when Jeanne was nine years old, her mother took her to a fortune-teller who predicted that young Jeanne would someday "reign over the heart of a king." So to help her daughter become the next big thing, Jeanne's mom (and baby daddy) provided Jeanne with the best education that money could buy. She was taught dancing, art, literature, theater, and other subjects—becoming a brilliant, dangerous little badass.

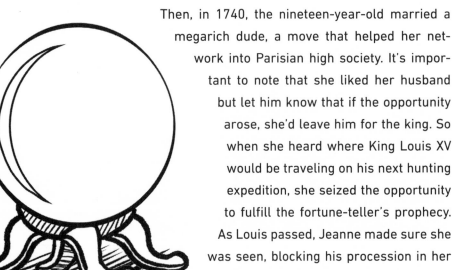

Then, in 1740, the nineteen-year-old married a megarich dude, a move that helped her network into Parisian high society. It's important to note that she liked her husband but let him know that if the opportunity arose, she'd leave him for the king. So when she heard where King Louis XV would be traveling on his next hunting expedition, she seized the opportunity to fulfill the fortune-teller's prophecy. As Louis passed, Jeanne made sure she was seen, blocking his procession in her bright pink carriage while wearing a fantastic blue dress. On his return, she did it again. Except, the second time, she swapped the colors to ensure her style could not be forgotten.

Enamored with this mysteriously colorful stranger ("ha—got him"), Louis insisted she be invited to the masquerade ball at the Palace of Versailles. The two hit it off; she became his mistress, ended her marriage, and moved into the palace. Because of her education, she was given an estate and assumed the title Madame de Pompadour. The physical romance between her and Louis fizzled, but she remained his most trusted adviser for nearly twenty years. During her time in the palace, her reputation for intelligent conversation made her a respected and sought-after dignitary. She met with philosophers, politicians, and artists—all seeking her intellect and integrity, and her not-giving-a-shit style of advice delivery; she was regarded as some kind of pristine therapist. Her life continued like this until she died of tuberculosis in 1764.

If someone tells you that your dreams are too big, hop in a carriage and wave goodbye to that bullshit. Or use that carriage to stop them in their tracks.

SUMMIT FOR YOURSELF

Not everyone is going to share your vision, support your goals, or understand your passions, pursuits, and personality. So what does that mean? It means, if you're not already, you need to become your own biggest cheerleader. And make sure you're living a life that YOU feel like cheering about (pom-poms optional). Set your own course, define your own purpose, and blaze your own fucking trail. Like Annie Smith Peck did—both figuratively and literally—as an educator, explorer, and expert motherfucking mountaineer.

Born in 1850, Annie was the youngest of four, with three older brothers. She attended an all-girls grammar school and upon completion aimed to follow in the footsteps of her father and brothers by attending Brown University. She was denied. Why? Because she wasn't a guy. (Fucked-up fact: Brown didn't allow women until 1891.) Disheartened but not discouraged, she decided years later to once again pursue higher education. Her father claimed it "proper folly" for a woman of her age—she was twenty-seven. She responded, "I certainly cannot change. I have wanted it for years." Her father changed his mind and agreed to support her; she enrolled at the University of Michigan, where she graduated with honors in 1878.

She went on to earn a master's degree and in 1884 traveled to Greece to study language and archaeology as the first woman to be accepted into the American School of Classical Studies at Athens. There, she became fluent in several languages while simultaneously discovering her love for mountaineering. Notably, she was the first woman to conquer the northern peak of Huascarán in Peru, which was later named Cumbre Aña Peck in her honor. This was just one of the many peaks she placed beneath her badass feet.

In between treks, she found the time to publish four books, act as the president of the Joan of Arc Suffrage League, and receive the Order of Merit from the Chilean government. Annie never married and blazed a trail around the world, summiting her last peak, Mount Madison, at the age of eighty-two. (She passed away at eighty-five.)

As another famous woman, Nancy Sinatra, once said, "Boots are made for walking." So feel free to walk all over those who don't believe in you.

HELL IN HEELS

Okay, moving from hiking mountains to walking in blood, let's talk about something scary. You like scary stories? Good, me too. Allow me to share one of my favorites with you. Are we going to talk about ghosts? Nope. The Loch Ness Monster? Thought about it but couldn't find any trustworthy sources. Children? Definitely creepy, but that's a lesson for another day. I know what you're thinking: "Captain, what could possibly be scarier than ghosts, the Loch Ness Monster, and children?" Well, I'm about to tell you: feet. Yep, the hand's awkward stepsister. Thank God you can hide (or at least accentuate) those disgusting ankle abominations with socks, footed pajamas, Rollerblades, and, most importantly, shoes. In particular: high heels.

Stilettos, peep toes, ankle straps, sling backs—it doesn't matter to me. I support that life and any other shopping addiction that helps you hide your fucking toes. Hell, I don't mind seeing a guy wearing heels. In fact, I might even throw a compliment or two his way: "Sweet calves, bro." A calf compliment is rather appropriate because calves (and other cattle) fit seamlessly into this high-heeled tale I'm about to tell you.

Why? Because high heels were originally invented by Egyptian butchers to keep their feet clean as they walked through the blood pools of slaughtered beasts. Yes, long before heels were being worn by drunk girls stumbling through piles of club confetti, Egyptians were wearing them to power walk through blood and guts. This backstory might explain why your girlfriend often feels the need to use her shoes as a weapon. It also doesn't hurt that the word "stiletto" is taken from a style of knife blade made popular in Italy during the Middle Ages. Huh, so high heels were invented by butchers and later named after a fucking weapon? Suddenly everything's starting to make sense.

Dating back to 3500 BC (some records indicate as early as 4000 BC), the original Egyptian heels were more reminiscent of the modern-day wedge. The more traditional version of high heels was first worn by Mongolian horsemen and later by cavalry riders during the Middle Ages, because the heels helped them secure their feet into the stirrups (kind of like cowboy boots). Imagine Genghis Khan, one of the most ruthless motherfuckers of all time, riding into your town wearing some red bottoms. Even if he decided not to burn down your village, his smoldering hot sense of fashion would certainly have been enough to start a fire.

Anyway, royalty (a.k.a. old-timey celebrities) eventually started wearing heels as a fashion statement, making the shoes a symbol of style rather than murder. Although, anyone who can walk in six-inch heels is still a serial killer in my book—and this is *my* book.

PRINCESS PROGRESS

You don't want to be remembered as "ordinary." Whether in the bedroom or in the kitchen, at the office or on the runway—ordinary is boring, basic, and fucking forgettable. Nobody has ever done something significant with an ordinary mind-set, and who says you can't walk into the office still wearing Friday night's fishnets? If you want to leave your mark, don't be afraid to break the mold. Be like Princess Pingyang.

As daughter of Li Yuan (duke, military commander, and descendent of one of China's original Sixteen Kingdoms), Pingyang was born in the spotlight. She very easily could have just settled in and become the typical spoiled rich kid, but she wasn't enticed by that silver-spoon princess life. She was just as clever and cunning as she was wealthy and stunning. So in 617, when her father declared war against the corrupt Sui dynasty, you better believe she was ready to revolt alongside him. Okay, she initially fled to avoid capture when the war broke out, but as any dude with a girlfriend knows, she went into the other room only to give herself time to plan a brutal retaliation.

While "hiding," Pingyang gathered weapons, war supplies, and soldiers. She also convinced other military leaders to join her and bring their armies with them. She assembled and led seventy thousand men, known as the Army of the Lady, crushing any town still loyal to the Sui dynasty. She met up with her father, and together they wiped out all trace of the former regime. In 618, the duo established the Tang dynasty, which went on to become the second strongest dynasty in Chinese history. And all this would not have been possible without Pingyang and her hard-hitting attitude.

Sadly, she died of "unknown causes" just a few years into Tang dynasty rule, but she became the ONLY woman in feudal Chinese history to be given a full military burial. When patriarchal leaders opposed this high-ranking honor, her father (now the new emperor) simply said, "She was no 'ordinary' woman."

What are you waiting for? Get out there and create some unordinary history of your own—start by getting arrested at brunch or something.

TAKE IT BACK

Revenge. I get it, getting dumped fucking sucks, and the desire to get even is understandable. However, relationship retribution is rarely worth your time. Why? Because the amount of time you spend obsessing over it almost never matches up to the temporary satisfaction that posting a jealousy-inducing selfie or keying a car might bring. I know this is the place where I should continue to tell you why it's pointless to remain vengeful after a breakup, but that would make this story rather boring. So if you insist on getting even, channel your inner Gwen and REALLY get even.

During the eleventh century, Queen Gwendolen, wife of King Locrinus of the Britons, found herself in the very situation that I just described: She got dumped. How does a queen get dumped, you ask? Well, it turns out Locrinus had been slippery with his dick for nearly seven years with a Germanic mistress by the name of Estrildis (with whom he'd also fathered a child). And one day, he decided to leave Gwen and make Estrildis the new queen. Essentially leaving Gwen with nothing. No alimony. No severance pay. Not even a positive referral on her résumé.

As expected, Gwen wasn't about that life. So rather than have absolutely nothing, she opted to take fucking everything.

She returned to her homeland, assembled an army, and waged war against her cheating ex—successfully, I might add. She killed him in a battle at the River Stour.

Then, leaving nothing to negotiation, she had Estrildis and her bloodline drowned in the river. And just like that, Gwen became Queen Gwendolen for the second time. And now that she was single and not looking to mingle, she became one of the first queens regnant in recorded history. She ruled as a respected leader, given her retaliation and clear demonstration of her willingness to seek revenge.

Now, dudes, if you even begin to think for a second that your wife or girlfriend isn't capable of completely destroying your life if you wrong her, you're wrong, buddy. Every girl has a little Gwen in her. Trust me. Her shit can easily go bananas: B-A-N-A-N-A-S. (Sorry, wrong Gwen.)

CARDIO IS FUCKING HARDIO

Speaking of breakups, what better way to deal with heartbreak than elevating your heart rate? (Actually, there are tons of other ways to do it, but this seems to be a go-to strategy for many.) That's right, I'm talking about the good ol' go-to-the-gym-every-day method of mending a broken heart and developing a killer body in the process. But no matter your motive, we can all agree on one thing: Cardio sucks. Running is meant for survival, not any form of enjoyment. Running is a skill that we, as humans, developed to escape scary shit—like dinosaurs and arranged marriage. Nobody likes running, so don't be one of those people who claims otherwise. Because not only will everybody think you're an idiot; they'll also know you're a fucking liar. NOBODY likes running.

Seriously, can running possibly get any worse? Unfortunately, it can. Running at a gym on a treadmill is probably the closest thing you'll ever experience to Hell on Earth. You basically take all the shit that sucks about running, then you combine it with extreme bouts of boredom, other humans, and subpar ventilation. Oh, and then there's that weird space-time continuum thing where you get temporarily trapped in an alternate treadmill universe—a universe where every minute feels like a fucking hour. So why are treadmills so awful? It's simple. It's because treadmills were designed for punishment.

The first treadmill was invented in 1818 by the English engineer Sir William Cubitt after noticing most of the inmates in local prisons spent the majority of their time just standing around, hanging out, and, well, not really being punished for their crimes. His initial invention was a series of steps that rotated at a slight angle around a vertical pole, replicating an endless staircase. These were installed in several prisons and used throughout the nineteenth century for two reasons: punishment and production. Prison treadmills were rigged to punish, but also harness the motion created by sweaty inmates to grind grain, collect water, and do other millworky-type things. Get it? "Tread," another word for walk or stride, plus the word "mill," to represent the work that was being done—and you have "treadmill." (Personally, I think "Endless Walk of Shame Machine" would have been equally as appropriate for his creation. But what do I know? I'm a writer, not an engineer.)

Anyway, eventually some dude noticed how ripped all the prisoners were getting and realized that treadmills were probably good for weight loss, health, and other things. And the first patent for a "training machine" was issued in 1913.

Now, if you woke up early today to go running, good for you—as long as you admit it fucking sucked.

BORN TO KILL

Cold, calculated, patient, deliberate. No, I'm not describing a serial killer—I'm describing your girlfriend. Albeit, the characteristics of girlfriends and serial killers are eerily similar. I know this, you know this, and the Soviets knew it back in the 1940s.

You see, during WWII, the Red Army recognized the close correlation between women and serial killers, so they began to heavily recruit women to become snipers. And they were right to do so. Women were fucking naturals at that shit. They'd hand a gal a gun and tell her to pretend that every Nazi soldier was her ex-boyfriend. Basically, anyone on the wrong end of her rifle didn't stand a chance. It was like handing a shark a fucking chain saw and telling it to go make some sushi: It was a bloodbath. I mean, if you think your girlfriend is cunning and patient now because she'll wait thirteen hours to pick a fight with you about something you said earlier in the day, imagine how cunning and patient she'd be in a life-or-death situation. Yeah, it's fucking sketchy. But also, it's pretty fucking awesome because tough girls are rad. During the war, the Soviets enlisted 2,484 female snipers. Who, together, killed an estimated 11,280 men—let's meet one of these ladies.

Allow me to introduce Lyudmila Pavlichenko, a.k.a. "Lady Death." Lyudmila was studying history at Kiev University when she volunteered for the Red Army in 1941. Think of it this way: While college students these days are taking it in the ass, both figuratively and literally—you know, with student-loan interest rates, weird boyfriends, and whatnot—Lyudmila was out cappin' ass. Just how many asses did Lyudmila cap? 309. Yes, three hundred and fucking nine. Her kill count rivals your bank account.

Lyudmila was the definition of a strong, independent woman who didn't need a man. Besides, if she had one, she'd probably fucking kill him anyway. After the war, Lyudmila even went back to school to finish her college degree, picking up right where she'd left off. This, combined with her military prowess, makes her perhaps the most badass woman to have ever lived. I'd wife her in a heartbeat if she hadn't died in 1974.

Guys, let this war story be a lesson to you: Your girlfriend was born with the ability to fucking kill you. So be nice.

DEEP THOUGHTS, DIRTY LOVERS

Google the definition of "power couple" and you'll read this: "Two people who are each influential or successful in their own right." Nowhere does it state that you have to be movie stars, rappers, or Instagram thirst-trappers. Sure, you can be, but all a power couple really needs is mutual respect and equality. Maybe you're equally as creative, equally as intelligent, or equally as adventurous. Maybe you're both just equally as fucked up. It doesn't matter what you share, as long as you share something. To prove it, let's take a field trip back to around 350 BC to meet Hipparchia, who was born in Maroneia—a small village in Greece, where not much happened.

Later in life, Hipparchia moved to Athens, where she met Crates of Thebes, heir to a massive fortune that he gave away to instead live on the streets and practice Cynicism (a philosophical pursuit requiring the denouncement of wealth, status, and personal gain). Essentially, he became a handsome-ass, dirty homeless dude—and Hipparchia was INTO IT. Her family, not so much. She wanted to marry him, but her parents continued to disapprove, so she threatened to kill herself.

Desperate to talk some sense into her, the family asked Crates to come over to speak with her, because they knew he wasn't exactly into the idea of marriage either. Instead, he decided to strip naked in front of everyone and more or less said, "This is all I have to offer. If you're still down, let's hitch up." They were immediately married—damn, Crates must have had a nice dick—and they quickly became the power couple of both poverty and philosophy.

They lived, taught, and fucked in the streets (literally). Not only did they upset people with their very public visits to Pound Town, but Hipparchia's philosophical prowess also began to piss off male philosophers around town. One dickhead even stated, "She belongs on the loom doing woman's work." But that didn't stop either side of the power couple HIP-C from doing their thing: Crates continued to write countless epistles, and Hipparchia became the only female philosopher included in the Greek text *Lives and Opinions of Eminent Philosophers*. (The *Hipparchia* genus of European butterfly was even named after her.)

Now, if reading this hasn't motivated you to go find someone worth having sex in public with, you should—if you haven't already.

BOOZY BOTANY

Your legacy—what is it going to be? More importantly, what do you WANT it to be? What are you going to do today to contribute to your life's story? Because every day, every action—every move you make and everything you say—has the potential to either contribute to or take away from your reputation. Think of it this way: Every deed is a seed. It might seem small and meaningless today, but with time, those seeds are going to become the trees by which you are remembered. And if you want to be remembered long after you die, plant seeds that make a difference. Like Johnny Appleseed did. Yeah, he was a real dude, but you were straight-up fucking lied to.

Sure, he was a naturalist and an overall nice guy, but he wasn't planting trees to fight America's hunger; he was planting trees to keep America from being sober. Born in Massachusetts in 1774, John Chapman was the son of a farmer and left home at age eighteen to begin his westward expedition. At the time, laws allowed a person to claim ownership of any land they developed or cultivated. So how did John claim land? Duh, he planted trees, leaving his mark on the areas he wanted. (Kind of like a name tattoo on a lover.) Once the orchards developed, the apples were used for the production of alcohol. Why? Because water at the time was unsanitary shit, so everybody was drinking hard cider and getting lit. And John was happy to keep the trees growing and the good times flowing.

More trees meant more money, which meant more American honeys. (Ignore that last part; the only thing John cared about more than his apples was his abstinence. He was too busy planting trees to worry about pleasing ladies.)

Anyway, in the early 1800s, he adopted the nickname Johnny Appleseed and continued to build his land-baron legacy until his death in 1845, leaving behind his 1,200 acres of booze-making botany to his sister. Unfortunately, the National Prohibition Act, which took effect in 1920, led to the destruction of his remaining orchards to prevent any further alcohol production. And that's when the bullshit story of him feeding, instead of intoxicating, America began.

After you finish this book (you're almost there), start planting your legacy. If you're not sure what you want that legacy to be yet, have a few drinks to help yourself think—Johnny would approve.

LOOK THE PART

Life's not fair. Life is what you make it, opportunities are yours to be created, and playing by the rules is fucking overrated. Society needs rule-breakers. Rule-breakers are originators, freethinkers, and pathfinders. Rule-breakers don't give a fuck, rule-breakers are not afraid to push their luck, and, most importantly, rule-breakers prevent society from becoming stuck. Without rule-breakers, we'd all be fucking fucked.

Take, for example, Robert Shurtleff—ever heard of him? Probably not. Because he didn't exist; this was the fake name used by Deborah Sampson to make shit happen. Born in 1760, Deborah had a less-than-glamorous childhood: Her father abandoned the family, she had no formal schooling, and she spent her teenage years in indentured servitude. At eighteen, she was free to go, using everything she'd taught herself to make a living as a weaver, a woodworker, and even a schoolteacher. (She wasn't allowed to go to school as a servant, so she educated herself using the homework from the children of the family she was serving.) In 1782, twenty-two-year-old Deborah wanted to join the Revolutionary War.

At the time, only dickheads were allowed to die for their country. So she dressed as a man, but her disguise was unsuccessful. Later the same year, she tried again, doing a much better job as "Robert Shurtleff." And due to her being five feet nine, she was selected for an elite infantry team, making her the first woman ever to serve in an American military unit. In her first battle, she was shot twice in the leg, but rather than risk a doctor discovering her true identity, she used a knife to remove one of the musket balls herself. (The other ball stayed in her thigh as a souvenir.)

She fought for seventeen battle-filled months before becoming sick enough to require hospitalization. And this is when a medic discovered her boobs and overall lack of being a dude. However, he respected her badassery, so he helped her receive an honorable discharge from the army. Then her next battle began: She was denied a military pension for not being a man. But she wasn't a quitter, and thirty-three years later, she got all the money owed to her. Deborah remained a rule-breaker until 1827, when she died of yellow fever.

Anyway, you probably don't need to disguise your identity, but we can all learn from Deborah's big dick energy.

LAUGHING ALL THE WAY

A sense of humor is critical to your survival. Sure, you need food, water, shelter, and other stuff like that, but a sense of humor is what holds your shit together when life is being a motherfucker. And what could be more motherfucking annoying than being kidnapped?

Now, I like to think I'm fairly "unkidnappable." You know, not capable of being kidnapped on account of my height, weight, and general lack of cooperation. But if I ever were taken away, I'd also like to think I could handle it as sarcastically and humorously as Julius Caesar. You see, in 75 BC, Julius was kidnapped by Cilician pirates and taken out to sea. (Not a typo. Cilician is different from Sicilian; don't try to correct me because you passed fifth-grade geography.) Anyway, when the pirates demanded a ransom of twenty talents of silver—which, at the time I'm writing this, is worth about $310,000 with today's silver prices—for his return, Julius laughed and told them to ask for fifty talents because they were unaware of his real value. And he even offered to get the fortune for them.

Julius sent a messenger to his homies back in Rome, but since they didn't have mobile banking back then, it took a few weeks to receive payment, leaving Julius with some time to kill. So for the next thirty-eight days, Julius kicked back and demonstrated a fantastically fake case of Stockholm syndrome. Not only did Julius participate in all their piratey games; he even wrote poetry and performed for them. He was the life of the party, and his captors grew to admire his wit, humor, and leadership. They became his loyal fanboys and treated him as a comrade and not a captive—despite the fact that he repeatedly told them that he would make them regret kidnapping him. Sadly, every good party must come to an end; the ransom was paid, and Julius was free to go. (In the nick of time too, because he was running out of jokes to tell.)

And what did Julius do next as a newly freed man? Well, he didn't become the father of Rome in 49 BC by allowing pirates to get away with shit like this in his twenties. Julius went home, gathered a fleet, and sailed back to the island, where he believed the freedom-seizing heathens would still be. And he was right. He repossessed the ransom, sunk their ships, and brought them back to prison in Pergamon, where they were punished and ultimately sentenced to death. I guess they should have laughed at more of his jokes, huh?

So let this be a lesson: Humor is fucking important. If your friend tells a joke, laugh, even if it's not funny, because one day they might have the power to kill you. And vice versa—keep track of those who don't laugh at your hilarious comments.

EAT, DRINK, AND THANK EVA

There's so much more to life than money. Sure, financial goals might get you up in the morning, but you need a passion other than profits to give your life some meaning.

Take, for example, Eva Ekeblad, born in Stockholm in 1724. Her father was a statesman, her mother was a countess, and her entire family was, well, incredibly fucking wealthy. In 1740, she married a count of equally not-so-humble beginnings (they were gifted two castles at their wedding). Together, they had seven children, owned several businesses, and socialized among Sweden's elite. It was some *Real Housewives of Old-Timey Stockholm* type of shit.

But Eva wasn't a drama-thirsty dame designed for television; she was a goal-oriented gal with scientific aspirations. In addition to managing multiple estates and being a single-ish mom while her husband was away, Eva used her spare time to pursue her passion for chemistry and new discovery. In 1746, at the age of twenty-two—six years and two kids into her marriage—she single-handedly reduced hunger in her country. How?

By making alcohol from potatoes. Yep, the best use of everybody's most beloved versatile vegetable was all Eva's doing. Thanks to her, potatoes can be both fries and the cause of a good night gone awry. Prior to her findings, grains were the base of alcohol creation, but Eva's boozy breakthrough allowed these crucial items to be used for bread and other substantial foods.

This dramatically changed the Swedish diet and over the years saved thousands from famine.

In 1748, for her contributions in both reducing hunger and inducing hangovers (good thing everybody now had bread to provide a solid base before getting absolutely shitfaced), Eva became the first woman ever inducted into the Royal Swedish Academy of Sciences. She later went on to develop nontoxic cosmetics using potato flour, as well as a safe way to bleach fabrics using soap. Damn—booze, beauty, and bright whites? Eva was the motherfucking pioneer of self-care.

So raise a glass and let's toast Eva's ghost. (Get it, "toast"? Because, thanks to her, everybody was drinking AND eating bread . . . Never mind.)

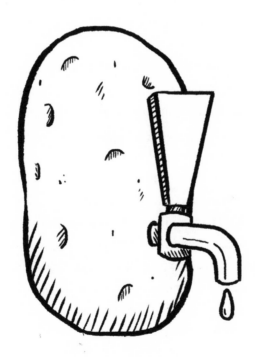

HUNG, IN MORE WAYS THAN ONE

Death and sex: two things that all of us will experience. The first, only once. The latter, hopefully, at least twice.

Let's begin with death: We all know it's going to happen someday—I mean, it's far more guaranteed than losing your virginity. But if faced with a life-or-death decision, what would you actually be willing to die for? Think about this for a minute. Your friends? Your family? Your pets? Whatever your answer to this, I believe you when you say you'd die for it, because some things are absolutely fucking worth it. And once you've identified what those are, you treat them differently. But what about dying for sex? Have you ever received dick or squished lips so fucking good that it was worth a meeting from the man with the scythe and hood? Chances are, you've never had sex THIS great—but if you have, please share your secrets in a book for all of us to read.

For the rest of us, here's a story of two people whose six-minute act put them six feet under (not by choice). In seventeenth-century Massachusetts, two Puritans met at a party: James Britton, a well-known "bad boy," and Mary Latham, an unhappily married woman with a husband nearly three times her age. Anyway, they hit it off and snuck into the woods to go rub some sticks together. (That's Puritan speak for being a freak.) And, well, they weren't as good at hiding as they were at fucking, so—in addition to the dozens of innocent woodland creatures—plenty of partygoers witnessed their infamous hump among the tree stumps.

Naturally, word of their get-down quickly spread throughout the town. And soon after, they were both arrested and put on trial. Neither of them denied what happened, and for this, both were sentenced to death by hanging. For their sake, I hope it was the best sex of their lives (or at least both parties were equally satisfied).

What can we learn from this? Well, the next time someone tells you their sex game is "to die for," don't fall for it. Tell 'em to take their lying Puritan ass back to seventeenth-century Massachusetts.

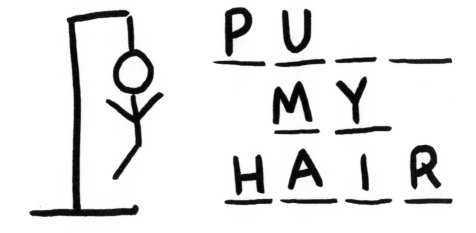

BEACH TRASH IN PARADISE

You want to hear the best love story? Well, it's more of a shipwreck, but it ends in love—you're going to have to trust me. And it makes *The Notebook* look fucking weak. The story I'm about to tell you involves a tropical island, a group of hungry women, and a sailor. It kind of sounds like a reality-TV show filled with drunk singles (the series could have the same title as this story), but the only thing getting lit on this island was a fire for roasting nuts—not chestnuts; although, this story does begin on Christmas Day.

On December 25, 1904, the SS *Herzog Johann Albrecht* sank in the Pacific Ocean off the coast of Tabar Island in Papua New Guinea, and a young Carl Emil Pettersson found himself washed ashore and quickly surrounded by cannibals. For the cannibals, I would imagine finding a young, fresh-off-the-boat Swedish guy on the beach is a lot like finding a breakfast burrito when you're hungover: love at first sight. But alas, this is still not the love story I'm talking about—even though the perfect combination of eggs, cheese, and potatoes wrapped in a warm tortilla can absolutely feel like love on a Sunday morning following a late Saturday night. But let's not talk about my dating life; let's talk about Carl and the cannibals.

Upon entering the village, Carl caught the eye of many local gals (I don't blame them—google him; he was a handsome-ass man with a respectable mustache), but one female in particular was crucial to Carl's cause. After seeing something she wanted, Princess Singdo asked her dad to please not eat the white meat from the beach. And like most dads do when their daughters turn the screws, the king agreed to spare Carl's ribs. Instead of becoming dinner, Carl became an honorary tribe member. In 1907 he married the princess. Shortly thereafter, the king passed away. And who became the new king? That's right, Carl did. From the lunch menu to the royal throne, Carl was living every dude's fucking dream. I guess Santa had something up his sleeve on Christmas Day in 1904.

Well, in addition to the many other stories in this book, you just read an incredible tale of love. Kind of makes your love life feel a little too fucking normal, right? In fact, I'm willing to bet your entire life doesn't feel anywhere near as eventful as anything you've just read—but that's okay. Because your life's not over. You still have plenty of time left to create your own chapter and earn your place in *Fucking History*. (P.S. I likely won't be around to write your story, so make sure you document your life well enough to make it easier for whomever does. Because all this research was a pain in the ass.)

ABOUT THE AUTHOR

Writer. Creator. Instigator. Not your dad.

@SGRSTK